Loving Resistance
and Resistance through Love

Loving Resistance
and Resistance through Love

A Multilayered Reading of Paul's Teaching
and Loving Testimony in the Letter to Philemon

ALEX HON HO IP

RESOURCE *Publications* · Eugene, Oregon

LOVING RESISTANCE AND RESISTANCE THROUGH LOVE
A Multilayered Reading of Paul's Teaching and Loving Testimony
in the Letter to Philemon

Resource Publications
An Imprint of Wipf and Stock Publishers
199 W. 8th Ave., Suite 3
Eugene, OR 97401

www.wipfandstock.com

PAPERBACK ISBN: 978-1-6667-0745-8
HARDCOVER ISBN: 978-1-6667-0746-5
EBOOK ISBN: 978-1-6667-0747-2

AUGUST 18, 2022 4:00 PM

To Adela Y. Collins, John J. Collins, Dennis Chan
and Steven J. Friesen, the mentors who helped me find
my pearls when I was still seeing only sand.

CONTENTS

ABBREVIATIONS

1 Cor   1 Corinthians

Gal   Letter to the Galatians

NIE   New Institutional Economics

NT   New Testament

Phil   Letter to the Philippians

Phlm   Letter to Philemon

Rom   Letter to the Romans

SRI   Socio-Rhetorical Interpretation

TDNT   *Theological Dictionary of the New Testament.* 10 vols. Edited by Gerhard Kittel and Gerhard Friedrich. Translated by Geoffrey W. Bromiley. Grand Rapids: Eerdmans, 1964–76.

WBC   World Biblical Commentary

Chapter 1

Introduction

1.1. INTRODUCTION: THE BEGINNING, AND WHY

In the everlasting novel *Les Misérables*, there is a scene that is very touching and has significantly affected my beliefs. It vividly articulated the transforming power of love. When Valjean was caught by the police because he had desperately stolen some silver candle stands from the same bishop who had helped him and given him food, he may have expected to go back to his life in prison. However, the bishop did not see that Valjean had stolen something from him, but saw the candlesticks as a gift to him. When the police asked the bishop whether he had given the candle stands to Valjean, the bishop's wise reply changed Valjean for his whole life. The bishop did not only deny the police's request but also gave two even more precious candle stands to Valjean. The bishop did not see Valjean as a thief but a beloved brother. He did not take this as an opportunity to condemn a desperate man but to transform a sinner. Valjean would never forget what the bishop did for him and the gifts he received from the bishop. It was a gift of love and with love.[1]

---

1. See Tom Hooper, dir., *Les Misérables* (Universal Pictures, 2012).

On account of love, the bishop gives all the candle stands to Valjean as a gift. There are two senses in which those candle stands are a gift. On the one hand, they are gift because they are made of precious material. On the other hand, they give Valjean a new chance for a better life. The bishop would be fully within his rights to see it as an act of theft. What is love in this situation? Love is not blind to sin but takes the opportunity to forgive as an opportunity for transformation. The bishop did not merely let Valjean go, so that Valerian would keep his sense of guilt and sin. The bishop forgave him and gave him an opportunity, but, most important of all, he gave new meaning to Valjean's life, with new possibilities. The bishop called Valjean "my brother," not a thief nor a runaway criminal, but a beloved brother. The bishop also reminded him there can be a higher plan for his life, and that he can be an honest man. Through the bishop's loving eye and loving words, the silver became an asset for a new beginning, and a criminal turned into a man who would sacrifice himself for a girl he did not know. This little girl became another gift in his life. The bishop's forgiveness transformed Valjean from a man of hatred to a man of love. How could a man possess such great power of transformation? Yes, this is the power of love that originates from our God and has been extended through his disciples who loved him and imitated him to us. So, what is this love? Unlike the Roman's love, or commercialized love in a capitalist society, God's love is not merely about ourselves but about our relationship with others. God's love is not about what we have but how we see others and how we respond to others' needs. God's love is not about us doing what we think is loving, but about wearing other people's shoes and loving them for their good. That kind of seeing is so important because it transcends our social values and prejudices and has us see others as precious as ourselves. Why is Paul's Letter to Philemon so attractive to me? It is because it is a love letter demonstrating God's transforming power. This letter is Paul's loving testimony about transforming a slave master by demonstrating how to love a slave.

Thus said, the letter has been misread for many years because prejudices about slaves had blinded interpreters to the message of love in the letter. There are two areas which can help you penetrate the core message of this letter. If we take into consideration Paul's thinking as demonstrated in his other letters, it can help better illuminate his loving message in this letter. If you understand more about the economic relationship between slaves and masters, you can better understand Paul's rhetoric in the letter.

The importance and power of this letter to us has been overlooked for so many years, and even centuries. Similar to Paul as he experienced the shortcomings of society in the Roman Empire, today we witness extremely poor people in extremely rich countries, politicians using all kinds of lies and propaganda to explain away all the problems originating from our social and political systems, and we witness people's selfishness wherein one hoards one's own wealth unlimitedly without seeing the need of one's neighbors. The message in Philemon is so important to us as we live under different types of suppression or witness various kinds of suppression and desperately look for a way to exert some influence on this situation. However, this kind of passion may lead us to fall easily into one of two extreme positions. At one end, if we are too romantic concerning the meaning of mission and hiddenly assume we may be able to transform this world, we will quickly fall into disappointment when we realize the structure and individual nature of the darkness. At the other end, we only focus on worldly darkness and human brokenness and forget our heavenly citizenship, and the resulting feeling of anger may drive us into hatred. In the Letter to Philemon, Paul demonstrated a loving testimony in which he did not lose his passion even when he fully understood the darkness of the slavery.

This book is intended to help you to read about the transforming power of love taught by Paul in words and demonstrated by his own action in writing Philemon. It is written to guide you as you read through the Letter to Philemon and penetrate the rich loving messages Paul has carefully crafted in this letter to address those deeply rooted values and prejudices toward a slave. This letter is about how Christians can pursue their own mission under a nearly unchangeable giant social and economic system. This book is written to re-empower you to find your own loving mission in this age full of giant suppressive social and economic systems. No matter where we are, we must have had some experiences of powerlessness under different giant sociopolitical economic systems. It could be a totalitarian regime or a capitalist system. The levels of suppression vary in degree and form but they are the same in nature. No matter what you call such a system, you can find some elements of slavery in it. On the one hand, I have written this book to help us understand the loving message and transforming power of the letter. On the other hand, it is hoped that reading this book will help you appreciate Paul's theological thoughts and the social context of the letter more comprehensively.

1.2. WHO IS THIS BOOK FOR?

This book is for those who missed the important messages of Paul in Philemon, and think that the Letter to Philemon is not as important a letter as Romans, Philippians, or Paul's other letters. Although it is the shortest of Paul's letters, it is also the most neglected one. Its shortness may also be the reason for its being neglected, because it may easily be misread. If you are not looking through the right lens or making the right assumptions as you read it, the letter does not seem to provide an important message. Unlike the Letter to the Romans, there seems to be no comprehensive theology in this letter. Unlike the letters to the Corinthians or Galatians, in this letter Paul seems to be very calm and is not addressing a very urgent and serious matter. Unlike the Letter to the Philippians, this letter does not bear so many golden verses. Thus, this book has been written to provide a lens through which the reader can see and appreciate the beauty of this letter and the right channel through which to hear Paul's loving voice.

This book is for those who think Paul is merely a theologian who isn't concerned very much about worldly problems. Many Christians do misunderstand Paul. As they usually first approach Paul from the angle of some summative theological statements like "justification by faith" or his teaching on baptism, it may give rise to a false or incomplete perception of Paul. Paul is surely a theologian, but he is not merely a theologian. He is a pastor, and most important of all, a believer who seriously acts out his faith. If you carefully read his letters, you will find they are full of pastoral concern, but are not limited to solving practical problems. He has in mind a greater worldview and faith. He hopes Christians can live out their faith in a world that is full of contrasting values and practices. He says more than once that it is exceptionally important for a Christian to have "faith working through love." This book is intended to help you witness Paul's actions in and through this letter. Paul's Letter to Philemon is not merely a message but a testimony of how Paul works out what he taught in different letters.

This book is for those who have a passion for their neighbors but feel powerless under the giant social and economic systems of today. Christians today who are living under the threat of a totalitarian regime like China, the power of the military in Myanmar, or the corrupted capitalism in the West may have similar experiences of feeling powerless. We all see the problems and the putrefaction of these giant economic and political systems. We also see how they use all kinds of lies to sustain their suppression of the poor and all those less privileged. However, we see no way out as we realize we are completely powerless to remove these existing systems through our own actions. This book is meant to help you to appreciate how Paul practiced his own teaching in Phil 3:18–20 that one must be a citizen of heaven in a worldly system in which the worldly citizens' end is destruction, their god is their belly, their glory is their shame, and their minds are on earthly things. Love is a resistance to darkness. Light is the enemy of darkness. We may not be able to overthrow the present system, but we surely can be a source of loving resistance to the evils of the system. Under the well-established and far-reaching system of slavery in the Roman world, to call a slave a beloved brother was a revolutionary act as well as a strong protest.

1.3. METHODOLOGY AND PRESENTATION

This is not an academic book, but a book originating from academic research. It is hoped that through reading this book, Paul's Letter to Philemon can be read in a new way and appreciated by more Christians. This new reading is mainly based on my previously published monograph titled *A Socio-Rhetorical Interpretation of the Letter to Philemon in Light of the New Institutional Economics: An Exhortation to Transform a Master-Slave Economic Relationship into a Brotherly Loving Relationship.*[2] As the title of the book implies, the book is written based on the methodology of socio-rhetorical interpretation (SRI) with significant input from the New Institutional Economics, and this is used to understand the values and the master-salve relationship that existed under Roman slavery. The SRI suggests that readers should read different textures of the text so as to understand the rhetoric of the writer. The core reason for reading different textures is that the "meaning" of a text is like a tapestry that is composed of different layers of meaning.[3] This methodology is basically still applied in this book, but presented in a manner that allows it to be read by members of the general public who do not have formal theological training.

Each chapter of this book will have four sections elucidating different layers of the text. I will use different scenes from *Les Misérables* to introduce the key theme of each chapter. For better communication with the reader, the script used is based on the movie filmed in 2012 rather than the novel itself. In section 2, we will conduct an investigation of the inner texture of the text during which the basic meaning of the text will be elaborated to include the meaning of some key words in the original Greek and some sentence structures that require our special attention. This is to give readers a basic and the most important starting point from which to penetrate Paul's message. It should not be too difficult to understand that merely reading the test itself may not illuminate the full meaning of it as Paul does not give an explanation of, or

2. Ip, *Socio-Rhetorical Interpretation.*

3. Robbins, *The Tapestry,* 14.

footnote to, every word or sentence he wrote in the letter. There-fore, we need the help of Paul's other letters to understand Paul's relevant theological thoughts, as he did not explain them himself in the Letter to Philemon. The third section of each chapter creates a dialogue with Paul's other letters and looks for Paul's theologi-cal thinking as revealed in those letters. This section begins with questions a contemporary reader may ask after reading the Letter to Philemon. Then, using Paul's other letters as a source, this book will present various theological thoughts of Paul that can help il-luminate Paul's teaching. This is equivalent to the intertexture in the SRI.

However, sometimes to understand what Paul is really ad-dressing requires an understanding of the historical context, and our imagination. This imagination is based on the letter, Paul's theological thinking, and the historical evidence. The fourth sec-tion is a more creative section intended to help readers integrate the text, Paul's theological thinking, and the historical evidence through a creative narrative. This narrative section aims to provide a platform on which the reader can visualize the possible relation-ships among the different layers of the letter. It is necessary for the reader to imagine for him or herself what was going on behind the scene. This is especially important for the contemporary reader as we are living in a world with a totally different system and values. In order to understand the message and the rhetoric in the letter, we have to use our imagination to reconstruct the original scene so that we can appreciate Paul's sentiments as well as his passion. With the narrative in mind, we can visualize Paul's actions, ten-sions, struggles, and love. Of course, the narrative is not necessar-ily true in the historical sense, but it is the most honest construct we can make based on our elaboration of the different layers of the book.

1.4. CONCLUSION

This book tries to help Christians to appreciate better Paul's lov-ing message for reconciling the relationship between Philemon and Onesimus and between Philemon and the world. This is like a journey for readers starting from the text and dialogue with Paul and then enjoying the beautiful scene by integrating the different layers of the text. It is hoped that through reading the Letter to Philemon from this new perspective, readers can gain the wisdom and energy to live out our loving passion and bring change to this broken world even though we may not be able to change the system in a short period of time.

Chapter 2

NEW LENS,
NEW RELATIONSHIPS

2.1. INTRODUCTION: REMOVE THE LENS AND SEE IT CLEARER

We have all had the experience of suffering from others' prejudices or hurting somebody else because of our own prejudice. In *Les Misérables*, Jean Valjean was not being seen as a human being, but a criminal numbered 24601. Javert was not willing to see this man apart from what he did. Valjean had just stolen a loaf of bread for his hungry nephew, but Javert insisted on seeing him only as prisoner number 24601.[1] No matter what promises Valjean had made and how many good things he did, even saving Javert's life, prejudice made Javert blind, and it makes us blind. Sometimes, prejudice penetrates our own life to distort our own images of others' true value, and who God is. The difference between Valjean and Javert is that after receiving the loving act of the bishop, Valjean reflected deeply on his life and chose to love rather than hate, whereas Javert chose to end his life when he found out that what he used to believe was wrong and the one he believed to be a

---

1. Hooper, dir., *Les Misérables.*

criminal was the one who forgave him and set him free. Prejudice distorts, and even worse, prejudice kills.

Unfortunately, we are living in a world full of prejudices. Politicians and merchants love to create all kinds of prejudices so as to manipulate us. In this capitalistic society, we are prejudiced to understand that freedom merely means negative freedom, and it is the supreme value in our society. No one else can take away our "private" property. We are trained to believe that in order to be free we have to earn as much money as possible. Living in an environment full of competition, we are conditioned to believe that poverty represents being a loser in the so called "free" competition, and therefore, the poor are not worthy of our concern. These prejudices not only affect our views of others but also of ourselves. Most important of all, they affect our relationship with God and our spiritual life. We sometimes think that our God loves free competition and tries to find winners to be admitted to the kingdom of God. Much worse, we use capitalist values to understand God's plans for us, and forget our God gave up his precious form of God and took the form of a slave. We wrongly think that building a bigger church is a way of glorifying God, but forget Jesus visits those who are poor, touches those who are sick, and eats with sinners. Sometimes, the worldly prejudices will hinder us from seeing our mission in this world. The purpose of this book is to help the reader to understand how Paul fights against these prejudices using both words and actions.

2.2. INNER TEXTURE: PAUL'S TESTIMONY IN WRITING THE LETTER TO PHILEMON

> Paul, a prisoner of Christ Jesus, and Timothy our brother, to Philemon our dear friend and co-worker, to Apphia our sister, to Archippus our fellow soldier, and to the church in your house: Grace to you and peace from God our Father and the Lord Jesus Christ.
>
> PHILEMON 1–2

In the first century, a slave was not only at the bottom of the social hierarchy, but was also considered bad and lazy. This kind of prejudice gave reason for a slave master to use all kinds of methods to control slaves including all kinds of, from our modern perspective, inhumane methods. So why would Paul write a letter on behalf of a slave? It would be very natural for people who were prejudiced toward slaves to assume that it must be a letter asking for forgiveness because the slave must have done something wrong. However, if you know Paul, who says in Gal 3:28 and in 1 Corinthians that there is no difference between slave and free for all of you are one in Christ Jesus, you would not believe that Paul would follow the contemporary values of his time and see a slave as inferior and necessarily bad. If not, what is the purpose of writing this Letter to Philemon? The letter has long been interpreted based on the runaway slave hypothesis. According to this hypothesis, a slave called Onesimus has done something bad, probably stolen something from his master, and therefore, has run away from his master. Somehow, he finally met Paul, who introduced him to the gospel, turning him from a thief into a brother in Christ. Now that Onesimus has a new identity and a status beyond the worldly status of a slave, Paul wrote a letter to his master asking his master to forgive him and accept this new brother in Christ into his household. This sounds quite reasonable and explains every loophole well, even though the letter does not explain this explicitly itself. However, a hypothesis being well explained does not necessarily make it true. I agree that this hypothesis can provide an explanation which Paul does not write out explicitly in the letter. That is also why this hypothesis is so attractive and why prejudices are not easily being noticed. They aren't noticed because they sound reasonable. However, the runaway hypothesis is probably wrong in three main aspects. Historically, this hypothesis can be traced back as far as the famous bishop John Chrysostom, circa AD 347.[2] Although scholars do agree he may not have been the first one to propose this hypothesis, he was probably the one most influential in making this hypothesis so popular. Scholar Peter Garnsey also

2. Ip, *Socio-Rhetorical Interpretation*, 6–10.

found out that Chrysostom showed great prejudice toward slaves.[3] It is not very difficult to understand why Chrysostom would hold this view, as seeing slaves as bad, lazy, and not trustworthy had long been one of the key ideologies under Greco-Roman culture.

Intertextually, some scholars have quoted Pliny the Younger's letter to Sabinianus as the supporting literary evidence.[4] The letter was a typical letter asking for forgiveness. Pliny the Younger wrote this letter on behalf of Sabinianus's freedman. However, if one examines the two letters more closely, one finds there are more differences than similarities. In the most important difference included in the letter to Sabinianus, Pliny clearly stated what had been done by the freedman and admitted it explicitly, and Pliny also agreed that the freedman was wrong. However, if we read the Letter to Philemon carefully, we cannot find Paul directly and explicitly admitting Onesimus has done anything wrong. Instead, in v. 11, Paul's mention of "he was useless to you" does not necessarily imply Onesimus was bad or had done anything wrong. Also, in v. 18 Paul's mention of "if he wronged you in any way" cannot be taken to mean that Paul is suggesting that he knows anything bad about Onesimus as he uses "if" in the sentence. These two verses will be elaborated more fully in later chapters. What we want to suggest here is that the runaway hypothesis is not as strongly grounded as we used to think, but only built on biased ideology and a literary comparison of two letters that are not parallel.[5]

So, what is Paul's purpose in writing the Letter to Philemon? What could Paul have written on behalf of a slave in the Roman Empire if Paul does not see him as a wrongdoer? Didn't Paul accept Roman slavery as a legitimate system? This book suggests that Paul did not accept Roman slavery as a legitimate system. However, he is not naive enough to believe that he can overthrow the slavery system by writing one letter. So this letter takes slavery as a given on the one hand, but tries to persuade Philemon to hold values different from those prevailing in the Roman world. In this book I

---

3. Garnsey, *Ideas of Slavery*, 72–73.

4. Knox, *Philemon*, 19–20.

5. Ip, *Socio-Rhetorical Interpretation*, 7.

am not going to list all the academic reasons like other books have. Instead, I will take readers through this letter step by step from a perspective lacking the runaway hypothesis and trying to find Paul's genuine purpose and passion in this letter. By doing so, I hope more people can appreciate Paul's loving compassion toward a slave who had the lowest social status in Roman times and Paul's loving action as resisting the grand and unmovable Roman slavery system. If we can appreciate what Paul has demonstrated through writing this letter, we could have more energy to face contemporary difficulties which also look so grand that we feel we may not be able to bring about any change to that.

We begin our journey by reading Paul's salutation in the letter. Unlike what many Christians may assume, the way Paul address himself, and the addressee, has already hinted at what Paul will focus on in the letter. Paul addresses himself differently in different letters. He addresses himself as a servant of Christ in the Letter to the Philippians, which carries a strong sense of fellowship in Christ. In the Letter to the Galatians, he addresses himself as an apostle with authority from God tackling the false teaching which may threaten brothers and sisters' faith. He calls himself an apostle of Christ Jesus by the will of God in his First Letter to the Corinthians, a letter in which he needs to use that authority to address the divisions in the church. These examples show that it is no accident that Paul chooses the title he uses in the Letter to Philemon, as well as the relationships he called upon regarding the recipients of the letter. So why did Paul address himself as the prisoner of Christ Jesus? What does Paul want to emphasize? On the one hand, it reflects Paul's current situation. On the other hand, Paul wants to emphasize his current situation as a prisoner is not because of the worldly system, but because he wants to follow Jesus. This is a very important message in the Letter to Philemon, that we are to follow Jesus even if we are living under the worldly system. We may find more of this kind of rhetoric in this letter as we start to read this letter carefully enough as guided by this book.

The second key message from this salutation is found in the frequent use of relational terms. How many relational words has

Paul used in this single verse? The answer is nine, including prisoner, brother, friend, coworker, sister, fellow soldier, father, and lord. There are actually even more to come in the other parts of the letter. So, why would Paul intentionally use so many different relational terms in one single verse? Of what does Paul want to remind Philemon? If we do not assume the runaway hypothesis is correct, we may better appreciate Paul's possible intention in writing this letter. Norman Petersen has also observed that Paul has used an exceptionally large number of relational words considering Philemon is such a short letter.[6] This shows that Paul was really concerned with "relationship" when he wrote the Letter to Philemon. Relationship has always been one of the key concerns in Paul's theology. If we take a closer look at Paul's relational terms in this verse, we can find that these relational terms remind Philemon of his communion relationship with others in Jesus as the head of this communion.

The salutation forms a natural reminder. It reminds the receiver about his relationship with the sender, and most important for Paul, his relationship with their Lord Jesus Christ. The first verse also reveals Paul's primary concern when he wrote this letter. Paul positions himself as a prisoner of Christ Jesus, Timothy as brother, and Philemon as friend and coworker. These are not merely relationships, but reflect Paul's view of others. They show the way Paul cares about his relationship with Philemon and others in the church. He also cares about Philemon's relationship with God and his relationship with the world and Philemon's relationship with Onesimus. How Paul designed the letter to use different rhetoric to ask, on behalf of Onesimus, for a new relationship, opens a new window to reading the letter. This window will lead you to see how deeply Paul is influenced by his relationship with God, and how passionate he was in trying to persuade Philemon to embrace this new relationship rather than follow worldly values. This is a very beautiful letter because you can see Paul's faith expressed through his action in writing this letter.

6. Petersen, *Rediscovering Paul*, 90–91.

2.3. INTERTEXTUAL TEXTURE: WHY IS RELATIONSHIP SO IMPORTANT TO PAUL?

Christians living in this age may not understand why this relationship is so important to Paul. We are living in an individualistic era; our private lives are our primary concern. Even salvation can be interpreted as a private salvation. The gospel seems to have no relationship with this sinful world except to recruit members of it to become part of us. An ordinary Christian may ask the following questions after reading the above section concerning the suggested new perspective from which to read the Letter to Philemon: Why do we need to care about our relationship with others, and especially those marginalized groups? Haven't we already got a ticket to eternal life? Shouldn't we be separated from this sinful world? It is well understood that our relationships with God and Jesus are essential to our faith, but why do we need to care about our relationship with others and our relationship with the world?

Yes, you are right in thinking that our relationship with our God is essential to our faith, but, without it, we cannot establish new relationships with others and the world. Merely reconciling with God is not the purpose of the saving plan of God. God has a purpose in saving us and establishing a new relationship with us. He does this so that we can establish a new relationship with the world and with others. This purpose also gives meaning and value to our Christian lives. It is the fruit of the new reconciled relationship. It is not just the condition of having the eternal life itself, but the meaning is part of the eternal life itself. Remember, Paul says in Rom 12:1: "I appeal to you therefore, brothers and sisters, by the mercies of God, to present your bodies as a living sacrifice, holy and acceptable to God, which is your spiritual worship." This verse is so important for understanding Paul's view of how our lives should be lived after converting to Christianity, for Rom 1–11 mainly discuss the saving plan of Jesus Christ. Chapter 12 begins to introduce how we should live in this sinful world given our new relationship with God. Paul starts to remind Christians about their new relationship with God, by saying we are living sacrifices. How we live is a sacrifice as well as an act of worship. The way we live should be a manifestation of what we belief and our new relationship. It has a purpose and a mission. Therefore, to have a new relationship with others and the world is part of God's saving plan. God's chosen plan is neither private nor exclusive. Instead, our gift from God is also a gift to others. Our new relationship with others and the world becomes a concrete way to actualize our Christian life and taste the fruit of the new life.

Concerning our relationship with the world, Paul consistently teaches us to live out our heavenly citizenship values in this sinful world. In Phil 3:19–21, Paul first condemns worldly values and practice by saying: "Their end is destruction; their god is the belly; and their glory is in their shame; their minds are set on earthly things." Paul uses four very heavy words to denounce those who follow worldly values and practices. This reflects how sinful this world is in the eyes of Paul. However, Paul does not ask us to leave this world, but to live out our heavenly citizenship in this world, saying in v. 20: "But our citizenship is in heaven, and it is from there that we are expecting a Saviour, the Lord Jesus Christ." Heavenly citizenship is the foundation of a new relationship with the world in which we should know that this world is sinful and we do not belong to this world. Although we may not be able to change this sinful world, our mission is to live out the heavenly values while in this sinful world. In modern times, we will see mankind having many giant problems and lots of darkness. Similar to the Roman Empire, capitalist society creates serious poverty problems and environmental problems for its own interest. Propaganda prevails and politicians lie and suppress all differing voices. We will easily feel frustrated, and tempted to privatize our faith so as to make all these problems irrelevant to us. Making the world irrelevant to us may give us a fake peace, but our lives will not have genuine satisfaction as we are not living out our missions.

Unlike our individualistic society, Christianity is based on relationships. Our satisfaction does not come from our own benefits, nor merely from our own achievements. Instead, our meaning, value, and genuine peace comes from loving our neighbors.

Although sin pollutes and breaks our relationship with God, and therefore also our relationships with others, Jesus rebuilds this relationship with love. This new relationship not only has theological significance but has practical importance also. The new relationship is rebuilt through love and for love. With the new relationship we should have enough power to overcome the values and norms of the present world. Both the ancient Roman world and contemporary capitalist society are grounded on selfish values. Romans saw slaves as merely tools, whereas people in a capitalist society see poor people as losers. Capitalist society sees the poor as losers in the so-called free market without realizing the rules determining the free market are unfair. However, Paul in Rom 12:16 teaches us to "live in harmony with one another; do not be haughty, but associate with the lowly; do not claim to be wiser than you are." Paul saw the need to connect with the lowly because he did not take the relationship created by the worldly system for granted. He not only asked others to do that, but acted out that mission in the Letter to Philemon himself.

2.4. NARRATIVE ONE: WELCOMING PAUL AND DESPISING THE SLAVES

It was a normal summer morning in a Roman city: extremely hot outdoors at noon, but still quite cool in some luxury houses where the wind was blowing in through widows that were well designed to capture the breeze from the Mediterranean Sea in the summer. Slaves crowded the market to buy what they were ordered to obtain for their households. They carefully chose the best products, since doing so might help them to gain the appreciation of their masters. On the other hand, they were very careful to avoid being cheated, since one mistake at the market might have serious and unexpected consequences. Some slaves were chained and displayed for sale in a specific part of the market. You could see the fear and desperation in their eyes. People were bidding for strong, young slaves. Some buyers were slaves themselves, and some were former slaves that had been manumitted and had become the clients of their former masters.

Knowing that Paul would visit his home soon, Philemon asked all his slaves to prepare for this great guest. He asked the slave manager to make sure that, when Paul arrived, all the slaves were in their positions and that those who were not in good shape were invisible so that he would be honored in the eyes of that important disciple. How could they become invisible? There were places specifically built for slaves in some large households or villas, such as the upper floor of Roman houses. In some poor households, slaves might live together with their household members. But Philemon's household, which was large enough for a gathering of the household church, must have had somewhere to cater to those slaves who were not in good shape, whose presence might not bring honor to their master.

Philemon, the head of this household, was very distraught throughout the whole morning. He wanted everything to be perfect so that, on the one hand, he could repay what he previously obtained from Paul. As he had received the gospel from Paul and gained eternal life from it, he must have to return something to Paul according the traditions and values of Romans. All relationships were reciprocal in nature according to Roman values; that is to say, he was used to paying something in return for receiving such a precious gift, and, of course, he expected others to pay back any benefit he gave to them. Besides, he really wanted to be honored by such an honorable person, because honor was such an important value for Philemon. He had been working very hard to gain more honor in his society; without it, he would lose many business opportunities, since honor was the key to getting more government contracts and business opportunities. Of course, Philemon was still using his old mindset to understand his relationship with Paul and the world. With these two good intensions, he walked with the slave manager to check again whether everything was in position. During the walk, he carefully examined every inch of the house and every slave responsible for every tiny job in the household. He checked the slave who was responsible for helping guests take off their shoes. He then checked the one responsible for preparing the guest room. Then he walked into the kitchen with a scowl on his face. After checking every position, he did not seem to be satisfied with what had been prepared.

When he went back to the dining room, which was right next to the peristyle garden, he sat down and asked the slave manager to come. Unlike the tense atmosphere, the room was very calm, with light and a cool breeze penetrating it from the window. The slave came and stood in front of Philemon without making a noise. He knew his master was very angry and unsatisfied with what he had prepared so far, but he didn't know why. After a long silence, Philemon said, "Do you know why you are here? Do you know why you are still alive?" The slave said with a trembling voice, "Yes, master. I am very thankful to you for saving my life in the war. I would have been dead if I had not been bought here to serve you. My life is yours, and you are my master." All slaves responded fluently in one voice, because this was their identity, and they had to be very clear; they could not make a mistake when their master asked them this question. Philemon responded, "Let me warn you once again. You are here to serve, and your value depends on how you serve us. If I am not satisfied with your service, you are nothing and useless to me. Also, remember the name I gave you. You are supposed to be 'useful' to me." Philemon said this to one of the slaves, whose name was Onesimus, because the sound of the name was very close to the Greek word for "profitable."

Chapter 3

FAITH WORKING
THROUGH LOVE

3.1. INTRODUCTION

FAITH IS THE FOUNDATION of our actions. Without faith we cannot receive the new life from God. Love is a gift from God. We have to accept it and transform our own lives because that is what the salvation plan is all about. Without faith we cannot receive love and become a genuinely loving person. Without love our faith will be in vain. The bishop, the important character in the novel *Les Misérables*, is not merely holding a high position in the church but demonstrates an enormous testimony of faith working through love. Holding a position in church is easy and does not necessarily mean that you are a loving person. You may have a doctoral degree so that you can teach theology. You may have twenty years' experience so that you can be the head of a church. You may donate a lot of money to a church so that you can be a board member of that church. All these can be good, but do not necessarily make you a good and loving person. Although the bishop was already holding a prestigious position at that time, he did not use the same eye to see others. Love kept his passion to see other's needs, value, and possibilities alive.

The bishop would have had all kinds of reasons to refuse Valjean or let the police take him into custody. Valjean was a former prisoner. He wore dirty and broken clothes. He was a disrespected person. Most of important of all, he did steal some silver from the bishop's house. What makes the bishop accept Valjean? It is his love. Love gives us the willpower to give up the norms and the labels and go deeper into others' lives. That penetration is powerful. In turn it provided the power for Valjean to transform and to become like the bishop. Similarly in our capitalist society, we have various "reasons" to be blind to all the poor and other marginalized groups. They are poor because of their own problems, including being lazy or foolish. In this free society, they are given a free opportunity to fight for their own lives. These "reasons" given by society sometimes blind us to others' needs and the problem with the rules of our society.

Faith refers to what we believe to be right, and love helps us to penetrate others' lives and touch their souls so that they can, in turn, contact our faith. That is exactly why Valjean was amazed at how this man knows that he has a soul when he was full of hatred and did something really bad in response to the bishop's kindness. This profound reflection and genuine dialogue do not come from the verbal teaching that we used to believe. The gospel or faith is sometimes transmitted, or works, through love.

3.2. INNER TEXTURE: PAUL'S PRAISE AND PRAYER

When I remember you in my prayers, I always thank my God because I hear of your love for all the saints and your faith toward the Lord Jesus. I pray that the sharing of your faith may become effective when you perceive all the good that we may do for Christ. I have indeed received much joy and encouragement from your love, because the hearts of the saints have been refreshed through you, my brother.

PHILEMON 4–7

Unlike what many Christians today believe, the thanksgiving section is very important in the Pauline letters. It is not there simply for formality's sake, but is of essential importance to the development of Paul's thoughts in his letter. On the one hand, scholar Paul Schubert is the first scholar to show convincingly that Paul has put the key words representing the key themes of the letter in each of his letters.[1] Unlike what they do in the contemporary world, people usually listened to rather than read the letters. Therefore, it makes perfect sense for an author to put his key ideas at the beginning so that the reader will have some psychological preparation for listening to the letter and be better able to catch the author's thoughts. Besides that, it is not merely a case of putting key words together, but of putting them in the form of thanksgiving, praise, and prayer. Paul putting his key ideas in his thanksgiving section may have another rhetorical purpose. Praising the aspects of the recipient that are related to the core request or teaching of the letter helps strengthen the letter's rhetorical force.

In Philemon's thanksgiving section, it is not difficult to identify those key words that turn out to be the theme of this section. Paul first thanks God for the recipients' love and faith. Notice, though, Paul does not merely point out an abstract concept of love and faith, but stresses their relational perspective by specifically emphasizing their love for all saints and their faith in the Lord Jesus Christ. The emphasis on the relational aspect of these two concepts is not random and is one of the key themes of this letter: "relationship reconciliation." To Paul, love always has a recipient and has to be understood from a relational perspective. We will discuss Paul's idea of love in the next chapter.

The next question then is why love and faith are so important to Paul? What is their relationship in Paul's thoughts? This point can be seen from the syntactical characteristics of this section. This section is syntactically linked together in a very close manner. The Greek word *akouōn* in v. 5 is linked directly to the subject, I, in v. 4. In v. 6, there is no explicit subject in the Greek and the translators of the NRSV, NASB, and NLT, etc., supplied "I pray" at

---

1. Schubert, *Form and Function*, 77.

the beginning of the sentence based on the adverb *hopōs* and the subjunctive use of *genetai*. This condensed grammatical structure provides us with a new clue to understanding the close relationship between faith and love in Paul's whole thought process. Paul first acknowledges that they both have love, and faith in Philemon and his community. Then he shows his expectation of the presence of their faith, using the phrase "sharing/fellowship of their faith." The Greek word κοινωνία (transliteration: *koinonia*) has a very deep meaning and multiple referents making it hard to use one word to translate its diverse meanings. It could mean sharing in a sense of believing the same vision together and fellowship in a sense of bearing with one another based on the same shared vision. Paul could surely imply both meanings when he uses this word. So when he praised Philemon's faith toward Jesus Christ and expressed his expectation that Philemon would further his faith, it was in a way referring to sharing and fellowship. This very likely implies that Paul wants Philemon to extend his faith to his fellow brothers and sisters, as the letter subsequently express this explicitly. This faith refers not only to things one believes as we are used to perceiving it nowadays, but also a motivation for actions. It is on that grounds that Paul hopes that this faith will become effective when Philemon sees the good things Paul does. What does Paul mean by "effective"? The original Greek word for effective is γίνομαι (*ginomai*) and carries a meaning of making something happen or bringing something into existence. That means Paul not only expected some conceptual change, but faith put into actions. In short, Paul has placed his ultimate expectation in a summarized form in that section as a prelude for his later request in the body of the letter.

The rhetorical function of v. 7 is more subtle. In the Greek, v. 7 is linked to vv. 4–6 by using a connective γὰρ (*gar*), meaning "because." It implies Paul's praise and expectation is based on Philemon's previous loving actions that have "refreshed his heart." What does refresh one's heart mean? We may not be able to comprehend the rhetorical function of these words by reading that section only because Paul indicates Onesimus who is Paul's heart σπλάγχνα (*splagchna*) in v. 12, and finally asks Philemon to refresh his heart in v. 22. By putting these three verses together, we may be able to read Paul's intention in putting his key agenda in this preparatory section. If the word "heart" really refers to Onesimus, what does refresh mean? Refresh does not have a very specific meaning and we will discuss that in a later section after we introduce the whole argument of Paul put forward in the letter.

In short, in this thanksgiving section, Paul has placed the key values he used in this letter to prepare for his main argument. Love is the foundation of the entire argument and Paul hoped that Philemon would manifest his faith based on love in his interactions with Onesimus. Many of you may have the idea that faith has nothing to do with our actions as Paul so emphasized justification by faith. So why would Paul ask Philemon to do something out of his faith and love? Is this thought part of Paul's key theological thinking? We will look into Paul's teaching of faith working through love in Galatians 5 to see what is implied in this verse and how this could help us to comprehend his theological motifs of faith and love.

3.3. INTERTEXTUAL TEXTURE: FAITH WORKING THROUGH LOVE IN GALATIANS

Many of us have focused only on what the Bible says but missed one of the key themes in the Bible; that is, what did people do and how did they do it. "People" here includes characters mentioned in the Bible and the author himself. If we investigate Paul's life and what Paul has done through reading the Letter to Philemon, we will find that his faith is not only reflected in what he thinks but is transformed into actions of love such as writing this letter on behalf of a slave. This is an action of love and an action with cost. A full exploration of Paul's sample as shown in the letter will be discussed in chapter 10. However, if we try to stand back a bit to read the letter, it will not be too difficult to see that Paul has acted out what he believes. He does not only believe Onesimus is his beloved brother, but he also did something for him and treated him as a brother because of love. Paul does not only ask for Philemon to respect Onesimus's freedom on account of himself (Paul), but also to respect Philemon's freedom by himself. So, the difficulty in understanding Paul's idea of faith, love, and action is rooted mainly in our misunderstanding of these concepts, or sometimes our under-understanding rather than misunderstanding them.

The Greek root for the word faith is πίστις (*pistis*). It is generally agreed among scholars that it is hard to find one English word to express the full meaning of this Greek word to translate it. It has sometimes been translated as "believe or trust." However, these two words "believe" and "trust" may lead us to an oversimplified conclusion that it merely refers to people's cognitive decisions made without the moral conviction of what one believes. This separation of believe and action may also be exaggerated by the Reformed theologian who places too much emphasizes the actionless perspective of grace. Scholars of the new perspective on Paul have shown that this separation is not historically true, nor did it ask the right question.[2] Action arising from one's faith is not merely a ticket to one's eternal life, nor is it separable from one's faith for Jews in the first century. Instead, living and believing is inseparable and therefore right action is the qualifier of one's faith instead of a consequence of one's faith. That view surely helps us to understand why Paul will say that he hopes his faith will be "effective."

It is not the purpose and scope of this book to give a full elaboration of Paul's use of faith. However, a short summary of its key perspectives will help readers comprehend Paul's idea of faith and its implication for Christian living. Faith comes from hearing the gospel (Rom 10:17; Gal 3:3, 5). Wolter emphasizes that in Rom 10:17 Paul's statement "faith is from what is heard" should be understood as faith is from what is preached.[3] Therefore, the meaning of faith is not separable from what is believed, as Paul says in Phil 1:27, "faith of the gospel," and "proclaiming the faith" in Gal 1:23. Speaking from a negative perspective, Paul also says in 1 Cor 15:14, "If Christ has not been raised, then our proclamation has been in vain and your faith has been in vain." The gospel is

2. Dunn, *Romans*, 344.
3. Wolter, *Paul*, 72.

not merely a doctrine but a story of Christ inviting people to join or participate in Christ. To believe this story is not only to accept that some concepts are logical nor to accept something is right. To believe the story implies our willingness to accept the gospel as a narrative of our lives too. Faith, then, is not passively accepting grace but actively participating with Christ. This view is confirmed by the subject associated with faith in Paul's letters. Paul uses "faith in Jesus Christ" in Gal 2:16 and "believe in Christ" in Phil 1:29. To have a full understanding of faith, we have to bring the content of believing together or else it would be an empty concept. Therefore, when we think of faith, we must remind ourselves that Paul is talking about believing in Christ's story, believing what he has done, taught, and demonstrated by his own testimony.

When we have in mind that faith has a content, we will be better able to understand why Paul could expect Philemon's faith to become effective and how Paul could talk about obedience to faith in Rom 1:5. This will be discussed in chapter 9. Paul Victor Furnish points out that "faith, therefore, is the acknowledgment that one belongs to Christ . . . and why the idea of 'obeying' the gospel can stand parallel to that of 'believing' the preached word (Rom 10:16–17)."[4] Faith in that sense is not merely believing some abstract moral principle but a decision to follow, and a decision to be part of a great community (koinonia) headed by Jesus Christ. It is therefore meaningful for Paul to write "walk by faith" in 2 Cor 5:7 and "live by faith" in Gal 3:11 because there is content in the concept of faith, but not anything in one's own thoughts.

With a deeper understanding of faith, knowing that Paul does use this term in a deeper sense and with concrete content in it, we can better understand Paul's paired use of faith and love in Phlm 4–7. It is not accidental, nor are those sweeping terms used without careful thought behind them. Instead, "faith working through love" reflects the core theological motif behind the whole letter. Paul has used this same pair in 1 Thess 3:6 and 5:8 and Gal 5:6. Among them, Gal 5:6 can express fully the theological connection between these two concepts in Paul's mind. In Gal

---

4. Furnish, *Theology*, 185.

5:6, Paul says, "For in Christ Jesus neither circumcision nor un-circumcision counts for anything; the only thing that counts is faith working through love." In summarizing the key points Paul has elaborated in the previous section in responding to the Jewish challenges, Paul contrasts "faith working through love" with circumcision. Circumcision is obviously a very complicated concept to be fully elaborated here. However, its Jewish identity marker function has been well articulated by James Dunn.[5] This marker is what people can use to identify whether one should be included in the election community. In Gal 5:6, Paul suggests that instead of keeping circumcision, one's identity should be reflected in their "faith working through love."

Faith working through love, therefore, is something that can be seen by others and not only something they believe in their hearts. Faith can be, and has to be, worked out because working it out is the necessary consequence of a genuine faith. As explained in the previous section, faith is not only a private action but a decision to join the body and mission of Christ. It is on this sense that Paul in Gal 2:20 says, "It is no longer I who live, but it is Christ who lives in me. And the life I now live in the flesh I live by faith in the Son of God." "Live by faith" implies living in accordance with what Christ has called us to do and demonstrated to us through his live. So why love then? What does it mean by through love?

Love has two aspects that are closely related to faith. On the one hand, love is the source of faith. On the other hand, love is the mission of faith. Love is the source because the origin of our salvation is God's love. It is because God loves us so that he sends his son to us to save us. It is a summative concept that reflects the intention and motivation of God's saving plan. Without love, we will have no faith. However, God's saving plan does not stop at individual salvation, a point which too many of us have misunderstood. It always comes with a mission. Love is what God has called us to. He first loved us and calls us to love one another. It is therefore as Paul says in Rom 13:8: "Owe no one anything, except to love one another; for the one who loves another has fulfilled the

---

5. Dunn, *Romans*, 356.

law." Love is not an abstract concept but can be worked out and be seen. "Faith working through love" (Gal 5:6) confirms our view that Paul has expressed his expectation of Philemon to work out his faith through the power of love as well as in the way of loving one another.[6]

3.4. NARRATIVE TWO: ONESIMUS IS VIEWED MERELY AS A USELESS TOOL

The big day finally came. Everyone in the house could feel that Philemon was full of expectation and anxiety. This guest was surely not a normal one, but exceptionally important to him. He really wanted to express his full gratitude to Paul and wanted to be praised by him in return, as praise from an honored person was worth more than anything else in Roman culture. The atmosphere in the house was very strange, as the silence did not match everybody's heartbeats. The silence was broken by an announcement made by a slave: "Paul is approaching! Paul is close." He made this announcement in the same way the Roman army announced good news concerning their victory—using the same Greek word we translate as "gospel" in our Bible—in front of the triumph, the long parade of the army, showing off their booty, including all kinds of luxury items and, most important of all, captive slaves.

Everyone wore smiles on their faces, but you could tell they were not really that happy, because one mistake in front of this important guest would result in very serious consequences. It could be physical punishment or being sent to the farm as a rural slave. This reassignment was not just a change in job but also a change in status, because being a rural slave meant that you had nearly no chance to be manumitted. Once you were out of the master's sight, your name would be forgotten, which meant you would be a slave for your whole life. This is not a burden one can understand today. It is not only life and death, because to some, a slaves' life may be worse than being dead if there is no hope for

---

6. Paul's full idea of love will be expounded in the next chapter.

manumission. Although every slave knew that not all slaves could be manumitted, there was still hope, which provided the incentive for the slaves to be "obedient" and "faithful" to their master. They obeyed and were faithful because of fear and fake hope. Their masters knew about their fear and their wish to be manumitted. Romans were very good at building; not just building grand cities but also institutions with different levels. The whole Roman slavery system was well designed and constructed based on fear and this fake hope.

It was that fear that drove slaves to do their best on their assigned jobs, and it was that same fear consuming their energy and humanity. Some slaves had already realized that they hadn't make a good impression on their master and were very nervous. Onesimus and his two friends, Chrestus and Aratos, were three of them. Their names were not their real names but those given to them by their master, expressing his expectation for them. Onesimus meant "profitable," Chrestus meant "useful," and Aratos meant "the prayed for." It was a tradition in Rome to name slaves either after their own name, to reflect their ownership, or after their expectations for their work. No matter which reason they were chosen for, these names have a common point: they treat the slave merely as a tool. They were owned by their master, and their value was intertwined with their productivity. They were human tools.

Onesimus, Chrestus, and Aratos became friends because they were all regarded as "below standard" in Philemon's household. They were usually assigned jobs that were not significant, and they had the least opportunity to be seen by their master. They lived in a house like an underground prison block, which is the worst place for an urban slave. Some slaves would live on the second floor of the house so that their daily lives were invisible to their master. Onesimus, Chrestus, and Aratos are disliked, but not because they really did something wrong. The responsibility went solely to those slave dealers, the most untrustworthy people in the forum. That said, they were experts in identifying customers' needs and making up all kinds of lies to hide the weaknesses or defects of slaves, making you believe that he had the slave you wanted. Unfortunately, once the master found out the slave had defects, like broken legs, or did not have the talent they wanted, their blame and anger would go to the slave and not the dealer. Onesimus and his friends were victims of this tendency. The slave dealer said to Philemon's chief household manager that Onesimus was good at accounting, and he therefore gave him the name "profitable," hoping that he could help the management of the household's finances. It turned out, however, that Onesimus knew nothing about accounting, which surely let the master down. His name, "profitable," became a scar rather than something with positive value.

These three were therefore assigned to work in jobs that were not significant and were invisible to guests. In this big event, they were assigned to help to deliver food from the kitchen to the dining room where Philemon would share meals with his honorable guests. Unfortunately, the bad luck did not stop here.

Chapter 4

THE POWER OF LOVE

4.1. INTRODUCTION

ONE OF THE GREATEST mysteries in human history is the power of love. We can understand the power of a gun, the power of money, and the power of politics, but how could love be so powerful? It is so powerful that some empires try to suppress people to love genuinely, where genuine love is relational, and substituting it by loving money or other kinds of fake idols. Love is not visible by itself, but we can witness people sacrificing themselves for others. Love itself is not vocal, but we can hear the most beautiful songs or poems reflecting the deepest love of humankind. Love is probably the most popular theme of Christian hymns or popular movies. What makes love powerful? How does love spread? Where does love come from? There is one scene in *Les Misérables*, which is the turning point of the whole story, where Valjean is transformed from a man full of hatred and anger into a man of love. In his self-reflection, he does not know why he suddenly feels differently, or more precisely, changed instantly after hearing the bishop's loving words defending him in front of the police. However, it is more than just words. It is actions in words. What the bishop testifies reflects his genuine attitude toward Valjean. He sees him as a beloved brother, a friend, and a man with hope and a mission. He is willing to bear the cost of Valjean's action. He just loves Valjean when Valjean does not believe he is lovable himself. Love is magical and powerful. It is magical because you can feel it but you cannot explain where it comes from. It is powerful because once you are touched by it you can do things you could not image.

Love is not discriminatory. Everyone can be touched by love as well as being able to love others. No matter who we are and where we are, we can be loved and be a loving person if we connect with the origin of love, our Lord Jesus Christ. Unfortunately, barriers to love are not absent. The most serious barrier we can witness in human history is putting all kinds of labels onto human beings to objectify them, thus isolating them and dehumanizing them. Labeling is the enemy of love because it blinds us so that we do not see another as a lovable human being, but as an object covered with different labels. It could be slaves as objects in the eyes of ancient Romans, gentiles in the eyes of the Jews, or poor people in the eyes of rich people in our own capitalist society. Once a label is established in one's mind, it can be very hard to remove it. Our view of these labeled people will be driven by the socially constructed content of these labels. For example, slaves in ancient Rome were viewed as lazy and merely tools.

The power of the bishop's wording is a good example of the power of love. He sees through all the labels that could have been applied to Valjean. Valjean was poor, starving, desperate and had stolen some precious things from the bishop's house. The power of love enables the bishop to see Valjean's humanity, his soul, and the bright future that would be possible if he experienced love. He addressed Valjean as an honorable guest, he forgave Valjean his sin, and most important of all, he touched Valjean's soul. How can we touch the souls of others? Many Christians have mistaken ideas about this calling. Some think that touching another's soul is to tell him or her the story of Christ, a shortened form of the gospel, and the gospel will touch the person's soul. Yes, that won't be wrong, but it's just not enough. The power of love cannot be fully tasted by hearing the gospel, but by experiencing it's actions and being on the receiving end of its love.

4.2. INNER TEXTURE: CHOOSE TO APPEAL THROUGH LOVE

> For this reason, though I am bold enough in Christ to command you to do your duty, yet I would rather appeal to you on the basis of love and I, Paul, do this as an old man and now also as a prisoner of Christ Jesus.
>
> PHILEMON 8–9

Paul surely realizes how heavy the ultimate request, to treat Onesimus as a beloved brother rather than a slave as implied in vv. 15–16, will be for Philemon. It is not only a rational decision, but also a transformation of his values and his attitude toward a slave. Paul does not only aim at asking for more humane treatment for Onesimus or merely freeing him, Paul wishes Philemon can be transformed and accept Onesimus as his brother in Christ. This would not have been easy. Having lived in the Roman world for so many years, Philemon must have treated Onesimus according to the same Roman ways and values as other Romans did. This involves a transformation of values and perception and it required strong rhetoric to move Philemon. Therefore, Paul had to move Philemon's heart rather than his mind. Paul's dilemma and his decision is clearly reflected in vv. 8–9.

Paul starts his formal argument, usually called the proof or the body of the letter in rhetorical analysis, from v. 8 using the Greek word διό (*dio*), which is usually translated as "therefore," implying the continuity of the following argument with the thanksgiving and prayer section. He then rhetorically states that "he is bold enough in Christ to command Philemon to do his duty." It is a very rich sentence, including several key words in the one sentence. First, Paul says he is "bold" enough. In Greek, Paul uses παρρησία (*parresia*) which usually implies confidence coming from one's position of authority. Scholars found that the use of this word can refer not just to one's position of authority position, but also to one's citizenship.[1] In the case of unbelievers,

---

1. Marrow, "Parrhesia," 433.

it will refer to their Greek or Roman citizenship. In Paul's case, supplementing "in Christ" with the source of boldness, makes it clearer that this boldness comes from the citizenship originating from Christ, which is the heavenly citizenship mentioned also in Phil 3:20. With his heavenly citizenship, Philemon is obliged to follow Christ's teaching, values, and model. It is this Christian obligation that supplies the power for Paul to say that he can command Philemon. The word ἐπιτάσσειν (epitassein), "to command," is usually used in a military relationship implying that Paul really wants to emphasize that he has the power in Christ to command Philemon to do ανηκον (anekon), "his duty or what he is obliged to do."

Amazingly, Paul says that he does not choose to use this power to command him but chooses to beg him to act on the basis of love. That surely implies Paul deems love more powerful than the hierarchical power he got. That is one of the greatest rhetorical sections in this short letter. On the one hand, Paul stated clearly that Philemon does have an obligation to follow Paul's command or request in this letter because he belongs not to this world but to the kingdom of heaven. On the other hand, Paul also stated that he can order him to follow and Philemon will have to follow no matter whether he likes it or not. This said, Paul chooses not to exercise this power, but begs him through love. Why? I think it is exactly because Paul understands that the core problem is not with the doing but with being. Paul can order Philemon to "do" what he is obliged to do, but Paul can neither order him to change his attitude, nor change his values. Even more important, without love, Philemon may lack the strength to do what Paul wants even though he may agree to do it. That is why he chooses to use love, because love is not only an argument but gives Philemon strength and a way that he can follow.

There is another rhetorical reason why Paul made this choice. He may have deliberately wanted to show Philemon an example in which love is more important and powerful than hierarchical power because Philemon may also face a similar dilemma, feeling the struggle involved in choosing between exercising power or choosing love. He finally has to make a choice. From this perspective, Paul rhetorically showed Philemon what to do through his own actions. It was not merely words but action. Through the whole letter, Paul made use of his belief in love as the structure and core of his argument. Most important of all, his love for Onesimus becomes the greatest rhetorical power in the letter.

Paul's choice and action may be difficult for us to understand for two main reasons. First, we are used to believing in something more concrete and visible like hierarchical power. Hierarchical power is very tempting, especially in the Roman Empire where all institutions were in favor of slave masters. Slaves were treated as objects and the property of the master. In principle, a master can ask his slaves to do whatever he wants. The whole social atmosphere places more emphasis on both military and hierarchical power than it does on loving-kindness. In the time of the early empire, Romans even lost the traditional virtues which they had valued highly during their republic period. The strong military power and highly power-concentrated political structure created an empire believing in power as their true God. Love, according to Paul's teaching and Christ's model, may have been seen as weak, foolish, and shameful under Roman culture, but is powerful according to heavenly culture.

4.3. INTERTEXTUAL TEXTURE: THE POWER OF LOVE

The power of love is not like the power the Romans strived for. It comes from within, not from external forces nor fear. It generates power, rather than utilizing the power of the one who loves. Therefore, we can see no limit to the power of love. Paul knows it clearly because he experienced and was experiencing the love generated by knowing Jesus. He says in Phil 3:8 that he "regard(s) everything as loss because of the surpassing value of knowing Christ Jesus my Lord." This reflected the reality that knowing Jesus will give one's life a totally new core value and this value can be summarized as love in Paul's theological thoughts. So, what is the nature and content of love? To answer this question is to give a full picture of love.

Nature of Love

Love may be the best-known theological concept among members of the Christian community. Love may also be the most popular theme for Christian hymns so far. However, it may also be the most under-investigated or sometimes misunderstood concept among Christians. The reason is that we have so many people talking about love. Love seems to be everywhere, especially during contemporary festivals like Christmas and Valentine's Day. Decorations with love hearts or romantic love stories on social media remind us that it is time to buy. Love in that sense pushes us to be self-centered and embodies a consumerist spirit. This kind of love is neither the love Paul referred to in his letter nor the love of God.

God's love is not the same as the world's love. New Testament writers follow the Septuagint's tradition using αγάπη (*agape*) to translate the Hebrew Bible's term for God's love. This choice of word is not ordinary at all. There are some other words that would be more popular that represent a similar human sentiment toward others. The most popular would be *eros* and the next choice would be *phileo* (φιλεω). These two terms were better known by people during late republic and early Roman periods. However, their intrinsic meanings just don't fit. Ερος (*eros*) refers more to people's self-love and φιλεω (*phileo*) refers more to brotherly love, whereas, *agape* refers more to selfless love or sacrificial love. Although there is still scholarly debate over whether this is the exact reason why Bible writers use this word, the deliberation over not choosing those other two words seems obvious. The further examination of how Paul uses the word *agape* can help us better understand why Paul follows this tradition, besides wanting to maintain the continuity of God's love.

Content of Love

To Paul, love is not an abstract concept, nor some term imagined by humans to describe a God made by human hands. It has concrete content in it. We can know God's love because God himself wants to show us his love. It originated from God's saving action (Rom 5:8). We can witness and touch God because Jesus came into this world, walked on earth, and bore our sin. He chose to be our slave to serve us and demonstrate how to love our neighbors through touching the leper, talking to sinners, and comforting the father whose daughter had just passed away. The love shown through Jesus' actions and Paul's articulation is something we can see, touch, and follow. It shows us both what God's love means and how we can live with love. These two sides constitute a complete understanding of love, so to speak: the origin of love and the mission of love.

Love is both the origin and the purpose of our mission in our new life as a new creation. God's love set us free from sin and its bondage so that we are a new creation living in this sinful world. We are no longer bound by our sin. Even more important, we are now free to love. That is a gift from God that has always been forgotten. In our individualist-dominated culture, we may sometimes see loving a neighbor as an extra burden or as an obligation which infringes on our freedom. However, this is totally wrong. In fact, they are integral to each other. They are both a gift from God, to be loved and to have the power to love. So love has two perspectives: one is freedom from sin and the other is the purpose of our freedom. This integral view of love reminds us that when Paul emphasizes that he is begging Philemon based on love, he is really reminding Philemon of the origin of his new life, his identity as a new creation and his new mission arising from God's love.

Love's Mission: Relationship Reconciliation

God's love is not self-centered nor self-loving. It is relational, reconciling us with God, with the world and our neighbors. On the one hand, it represents God's initiative, reconciling the broken relationship between men and God. It is not for God's sake but for ours. God's loving purpose does not end with the reconciliation of our relationship with him, but continues with him to be agents of reconciliation. After receiving his loving reconciliation and seeing Jesus's loving example, we can be filled with the same power of love and mission that Jesus had in this broken world. We can see this double reconciliation nature of love from the two commands emphasized in both the OT and the NT. On the one hand we are commanded to love our God wholeheartedly and on the other hand we are called to love our neighbors as ourselves.

With our new relationship with God we have a new identity of not belonging to this world. Paul calls people with this new identity a new creation (2 Cor 5:17). This new identity allows us to live free from the bondage of sin and this world and with a new loving mission (Gal 5:13–14). Paul clearly states that we are all called to be free not to serve our own ambitions nor satisfy our own self-indulgence but through love to serve one another. Therefore, we have a new relationship with this world. Formerly, this sinful world filled with all kinds of temptations enslaved us so that we could not live out the full values created by God. With this new identity, although we are still living in the same broken world, this brokenness becomes the subject of our mission. To be the reconciler in this broken world and to love those who are hurt by this world becomes our mission.

Loving our neighbor as ourselves becomes our mission in this new identity. Unlike some Christians who may undervalue the importance of the commandment to love our neighbor as ourselves, Paul says twice that loving our neighbor as ourselves is not an ordinary instruction, but the sum of the whole law. In Gal 5:14, Paul says, "The whole law is summed up in a single commandment, 'You shall love your neighbor as yourself.'" In Rom 13:9, after naming four commandments, Paul says, "And if there is any other commandment, are summed up in this saying, namely, 'Love your neighbor as yourself.'" Loving our neighbor is a summary of the whole law because it reflects the core mission of our new identity and our relationship with this world. Having been freed from the bondage of this world, we can act actively in this broken world.

Brokenness is no longer bondage but the target of our mission. Our brokenness becomes a valuable asset to help with healing this brokenness. We are loved to love and become the agent of love. With this new identity, Christians become a loving community not because we are very loving but because we are loved and commissioned to love. We still have our shortcomings and weaknesses. However, we have the freedom to love and a mission to love. Therefore, calling each other brother does remind us of our mission of love and shared identity in Christ.

Loving Resistance

This book is titled loving resistance and resistance through love. This may seem contradictory if we do not have an accurate understanding of love. If we understand the nature and content of love in the New Testament correctly, we can better comprehend a coherent picture of love and resistance. Love does not belong to the values of this world. It originated from God and is not self-centered. It freed us from bondage to this world and commissioned us to love our neighbor. These values are totally different from the values that prevailed in Roman cultures and from the values of capitalist societies today. To stand firm in our core value is resistance. To resist is to love. In the Letter to Philemon, when Paul begs Philemon based on love he is begging Philemon to resist the prevailing values and institutions surrounding him concerning how to treat his slave. Loving resistance is not easy. Sometimes, to love may be far harder than resistance through political and military means.

4.4. NARRATIVE THREE: CONTRASTING VIEWS; INSTRUMENTAL OR LOVING RELATIONSHIP?

When Paul arrived, his gentleness and kindness surprised everyone, including all the slaves. Unlike any other guests of honor, Paul greeted everyone in the household, including slaves. He not only refused to be served by the slaves but also talked to them. In his eyes, there was no difference between slaves and free people. However, this attitude did create a very awkward atmosphere in the household. Everyone could see that Paul's kindness exerted severe pressure on Philemon, the master of this house, who was used to being served and giving orders in the house. When Paul finally sat down and started to talk to Philemon, everyone in the house seemed to relax a lot. However, much worse things came during the dinner.

When all the guests and family members were readily lying on the couches that lined the three sides of the dining room, with Philemon at the center of the room and Paul next to him so that they could talk to each other, the slaves started to serve dinner. The dining room was luxuriously decorated with colorful paintings on the walls and a mosaic on the floor. The more colorful a room is, the richer the household should be. The reason behind this logic is that some kinds of colorful marble could only be found in some remote areas, like Egypt or Greece. The importance of marble to the Roman Empire can be seen in Augustus's famous saying, "I found Rome a city of brick and left it a city of marble." Dinner, for rich a household like Philemon's, was not only for providing daily necessary nutrition but also to show off one's honor. Philemon might have needed to show off his wealth and honor to Paul, but he surely wanted to show his love by giving him the best dinner he could.

When dinner began, the slaves started to take out the food that they had been preparing for a long time. They first served bread made by different cereals, including wheat, barley, oats, rye, and millets. The best wine was served throughout the whole dinner, as well as fruits. These are the basic aspects of the meal a usual family would have. A rich household like Philemon's had to prepare meat and fish for their honorable guests to show their respect. To receive Paul, Philemon prepared a whole pig and various kinds of fish, hoping that Paul would notice his passion to honor him, yet Paul seemed to care more about the slaves standing beside them than the food. He asked if they had eaten their dinner yet. No one dared to answer, knowing the truth would upset Paul and, most importantly, make Philemon angry. However, the hesitation already told Paul that they had not. It was not a problem for them, because all the slaves had grown used to having dinner after their master. Luckily Paul did not question them but asked all the slaves standing nearby to come to share the meal with him: "Come, brothers, share with us." Paul's words seemed to make the whole world stop. No one dared to make a noise. This silence was rare and strange, and everyone in the room felt the tension. Everyone knew how Philemon would feel when he heard Paul addresses slaves as "brothers." However, all the slaves seemed to hear the most beautiful sound on earth, because they had been treated merely as an instrument for such a long period, so they might have forgotten that they were human. Having heard that word, "brothers," Onesimus seemed to be awakened, and he started to take a piece of food from the table to eat, and then so did two of his friends, Chrestus and Aratos. They may have forgotten what food they ate, but they would never forget that moment of awakening with the knowledge that they were indeed human. They were addressed as human and treated as human. However, this awakening was dangerous, because the reality was that they were still being viewed as instruments. Even worse, there were philosophies justifying slaves' instrumental status by saying that there are men who are inferior to others by nature and that it is better if they are subjected to others who are superior.

Onesimus may not remember the taste of the food he just ate. He may not remember the details about what Paul and Philemon had discussed about love and brotherhood. His heart was instead filled with tension between being an instrument and a human. How could he be a human in this giant slavery system?

Chapter 5

SEEING IS RESISTANCE

5.1. INTRODUCTION

IN *LES MISÉRABLES*, there is a character who is full of tension and struggles, Javert. He is not a bad guy. He is loyal to his duty as an inspector and the law. You can say he is just doing his duty. Yes and no. It is his duty to maintain order but not his duty to see someone merely as a number—24601. It is his duty to trace a runaway criminal but not his duty to see one as a criminal even after he has served his sentence. It is his duty to maintain the law but not his duty to sentence someone to death. We are not only driven by formal duty. We are at the same time driven by invisible and informal rules including prejudices and all kinds of labels staked on different groups of people. Both formal duty and informal norms are potentially dangerous. They are not value neutral. Sometimes, they may become part of our core values through our daily practice of them. This unintentional penetration of these values is more threatening to our lives than any external impact because they enter our lives in such an indiscernible way.

Javert actually is a victim of the hidden values and norms of his society. He was unintentionally trained to be pitiless, seeing complying with the law to be the highest value and seeing people through the labels stuck on them, but not seeing their genuine faces. He sees no good in other's actions. He focuses on Valjean's lawbreaking but not his kind motives. Javert cannot even be kind to himself. He chose to kill himself after receiving kindness from the one he had been tracing for so many years. He wanted to catch Valjean and did not care what the result for the poor little girl Cosette might be. The hardest thing for Javert to accept was that he was released by Valjean, whom Javert sees as a criminal, even though Valjean had a chance to kill him. Javert found this kindness incomprehensible under his own rules. He could have, on the other hand, accepted that he had been wrong for the past few years because there is kindness and forgiveness in this world. His final choice reflects that he cannot accept that he has been wrong for so many years nor can he forgive himself. These values did not originate in Javert but were implanted through different institutions, both formal and informal, of our society. We accept these values in a rather unintentional way during our daily participation in these institutions.

It is sad but true that spiritual warfare is in our daily lives. There are so many hidden prejudices toward different groups, usually minority groups, of people. Prejudices include wrong perceptions driving us to see Black people as dangerous, Chinese as not being faithful, and Muslims as terrorists, etc. In the first century, people also suffered from similar kinds of prejudice. Philosophy, such as Aristotle's natural slave theory, and laws related to managing slaves, both rationalize the exploitation of slaves and even justify the seeing of slaves as property. We encounter similar labels and norms every day in capitalist society too. Just take a moment to be silent and think about how we view the poor, the minority groups surrounding us, and people holding opinions that are different from ours. If we are honest with ourselves, we may find that our views on these groups of people may also be affected by different labels or prejudices prevailing in our society. If we do not stand firm on our loving values, we may also fall into a trap similar to that of Javert, who got used to following the norms of society in the way he saw others and himself.

5.2. INNER TEXTURE: SEEING A SLAVE AS PAUL'S OWN SON

> I am appealing [am begging] to you for my child, Onesimus,
> whose father I have become during my imprisonment.
>
> PHILEMON 10

After the carefully designed prelude of the letter and both of the rhetorically and theologically dense verses, Paul directly introduced his subject of appeal, that is Onesimus. Onesimus is a very common name for slaves, meaning profitable. This name reflects the prevailing attitude toward slaves at that time. Slave masters viewed slaves merely as property or tools. Slaves had been objectified. Objectifying a slave was the result of both formal and informal institutions in the Roman Empire. Roman people were indoctrinated with this value through their daily participation in society. The value of a slave was instrumental only and that's why slaves were usually named as if they were a tool. Their value lay in their performance in the eyes of their master. If they could win their master's favor, they may be given some more important tasks which can give them a better chance to be freed. Conversely, if they were disliked by their master, they may be given some unimportant jobs or even worse be sent to a rural field, which implied they might lose their chance of being freed forever. Paul knows this Roman norm and values very well, which was not what Paul would have expected between people within a believing community. He planned his address of this prejudice well.

Paul deliberately uses the word παρακαλῶ (parakalō), meaning "I beg" or "am begging," twice), to emphasize his strong conviction toward what he is trying to ask for in the following letter. Before formally mentioning the name of Onesimus, he describes him as my child, ἐμοῦ τέκνου (emou teknou). The use of τέκνον (teknon) has two important connotations aimed at opening Philemon's eyes to see Onesimus as a beloved brother rather than merely a piece of property or a tool. First, τέκνον means child and is human not a tool. Adding this description before the mentioning of his name is not accidental. It is done intentionally to remind Philemon that Onesimus is not a tool but a human being. In any case, Onesimus is obviously not Paul's biological son. So, saying Onesimus is Paul's child is to introduce this new relationship with God and with Philemon. Paul always used τέκνον to describe our relationship with God (Rom 8:16, 17, 21; 9:7; Phil 2:15). Moreover, Paul strengthens this relationship in Christ by using the word ἐγέννησα (egennāsa), meaning "begot," to further strengthen Onesimus's new role. Onesimus, therefore, is Paul's spiritual son. They have a new relationship in Christ.

To hear the rhetorical effect of v. 10, we have to place ourselves back in the first century. Imagine that every slave master had the same attitude toward their slaves. The law permits you to treat them as slaves, philosophers tell you that you are justified in doing so, and you can observe that these slaves were sold as property or a product in the Roman forum every day. The force of this corporate practicing of the prevailing values can be so strong that it influences people's perception. It was so normal and broadly accepted that everyone took it for granted. In order to persuade Philemon to forgo this deeply indoctrinated value, Paul has to design his rhetoric carefully to open Philemon's eyes to see something he was blind to before. Verse 10 is just the beginning of the whole rhetorical passage reminding Philemon that Onesimus is a human being with the same relationship with Christ that he and Paul have.

How important is it to see someone as a brother? Is it part of the gospel to have the ability and mission to break through contemporary prejudice and see someone as a person of value?

5.3. INTERTEXTUAL TEXTURE: PAUL'S ESCHATOLOGICAL PERSPECTIVE

Having received the love of God, we have a new identity, new power, and a new mission to love. The values of this new identity are different from the values of the worldly identity. The Christian identity originates from God's love and is expressed through a different kind of love. Christian action is not to earn one's eternal life but to exercise one's power and mission. So the transformation Paul asks Philemon to make in the letter is inherently assumed in the new identity of a Christian. This new identity is sometimes called the citizenship of heaven. In Phil 3:19–20, Paul emphasizes the transcending nature of this citizenship so much. He uses a Greek word, πολίτευμα (*politeuma*), to describe this new identity. This word embraces a very complicated meaning. On the one hand, it could mean a privileged status, with lots of fringe benefits and rights, which the Roman Empire intended to establish so as to create an eagerness for Roman citizenship among other ethnic groups. One the other hand, this word was used to represent the group of Jewish people living in the Roman Empire as an independent state according to their own laws and rules.[1] The intention of Paul when he used this word is made clearer if we consider the adding of the qualifier "in heaven" to distinguish this citizenship as not Roman but belonging to heaven. The rhetoric may mean you have to do everything you can to get that citizenship, but not the Roman one.

Having a citizenship is not nominal but real; it will be reflected in every part of our daily lives. Roman citizenship was an identity that you had to use so much effort to get. Then, you would want to tell everyone you are now a Roman. You wear a toga so that others will admire you or your status. You can get into the Roman forum freely (some scholars have suggested that some Roman forums were limited to Roman citizens only) and do all kinds of business and make social connections there. As a Roman wearing a toga, you will also be visible at every event taking place in the amphitheater as the seats of the amphitheater were categorized according to social status. They started from the best seats for the emperor or the head of the province, through senators, generals, and equestrians, who were all Romans, down to other plebeians and finally slaves. The superiority of Roman citizenship was actually visible everywhere in the Roman cities. This visibility of Roman status was part of Roman policy in order to use that superiority of status to achieve the purpose of social control.

1. Hellerman, *Philippians*, 231.

It is on this grounds that Paul reminds the brothers and sisters in Philippians to "live in a manner worthy of the gospel of Christ," because how we live reflects our inner self-identity. Paul uses a Greek word, *politeuomai*, translated in the NRSV as "live in a manner," which can be translated more directly as "to behave as a citizen," to remind believers to live not according to the prevailing Roman values but to follow heavenly values. Seeing other believers, no matter their social status, as valuable and belonging to the body of Christ is surely one of the values. In 1 Cor 12:13 he says, "For in the one Spirit we were all baptized into one body—Jews or Greeks, slaves or free—and we were all made to drink of one Spirit." In Gal 3:27–28 Paul says, "For all of you who were baptized into Christ have clothed yourselves with Christ. There is neither Jew nor Greek, there is neither slave nor free man, there is neither male nor female; for you are all one in Christ Jesus." This oneness in Christ is a very important theological motif in Paul's thoughts. Eschatologically, we may still have different social statuses among members of the believing community, but we "see" others through a new value system. That is why, in Rom 12, after introducing the title of the following section in v. 9, Paul says, "Let love be genuine; hate what is evil, hold fast to what is good" concerning how believers are to put love into practice. This was important for believers who were living in Rome where Roman values dominated. In v. 16, Paul reminds believers to "live in harmony with one another; do not be haughty, but associate with the lowly, do not claim to be wiser than you are." Harmony is not possible if one sees others as lower than oneself, not to mention seeing others as a piece of property. We may not be able to change the social structure in a short period of time, but we can transform our own values to become heavenly values.

This is also true in our capitalist society. We have so many prejudices that are inherently implanted in our society. We have not only learned these values but have also been indoctrinated with these values through our daily participation of the institutions associated with our capitalist society. Our education tells us that winners in free competition deserve better opportunities in society, however it does not tell us that this education is not necessarily fair to those poorer families. The free market teaches us money is power and honor. Private property rights are sacred because once we infringe on others' property rights they will lose their incentive and all will suffer. As long as the "free" market provides an equal opportunity for everyone to compete, it is a fair system to be adopted for resource allocation. The prejudice created is that poor people deserve their inferiority because they lost in a "fair" competition. These prejudices help to sustain capitalist societies because they rationalize the unfairness of the society and allow people to live comfortably in a highly polarized and unfair society. Today, we may not have an explicit slavery system such as the Roman Empire had, but we are living in a society full of similar oppression and prejudice. In order to live in harmony, we have to beware of the world's values, and most importantly, the hidden prejudices with which we have been indoctrinated through our participation in games governed by the values of capitalist society.

5.4. NARRATIVE FOUR: INNER STRUGGLE; WHO OR WHAT AM I?

The more inner struggle you had, the worse you performed as a slave. Being awakened as a human being, you would not be the same. You might not be as obedient as before. There are two Greek words, ὑπακούω (*hupakouo*) and ὑποτάσσω (*hupotasso*), that we may always confuse. *Hupakouo* (Phil 12:2; 2 Thess 1:8; 3:14; Rom 6:17), better translated as "obey," describes people's wholehearted submission to authority or someone respected. That obedience is what slave masters require their slaves to show to them. Whereas *hupotasso* (Rom 13:1; 8:7; 10:3; 1 Cor 14:34) can often be translated as "subject to," which implies recognizing the existence of a power structure or norms and submitting yourself to these rules. At different levels of submission, your own sentiments—sadness or hesitation—may be shown on your face. Unfortunately, these human characteristics are not welcome in a slave-owning society unless you have a very good relationship with your master. Onesimus obviously was not one of those lucky ones. This newly awakened identity exerted great pressure on him. At the same time, his poor performance as a slave upset his master, resulting in an even worse relationship with him. He had no choice but to suppress his humanity again or seek an alternative to ease this tension.

During this struggling period, he thought of Paul. This man was not like any others living in Roman society. He was surely someone of high honor, but he did not behave that way. He did not come to be served but to care for everyone. He saw everyone as a human and brother. This man seemed to have the wisdom to solve Onesimus's struggle. Most importantly of all, he suddenly remembered that Paul had talked about something he had never heard of, called *agape*, usually translated as "love" in English. The Romans also talked about love, but they used other Greek terms, such as *eros* or *phileo*, not the *agape* that Paul used during his conversation with Philemon. Onesimus did not know what exactly this term meant, but he could guess how important it was from Paul's long and passionate conversation with Philemon. It was not only what Paul said but also how Paul behaved that led Onesimus to decide to find him.

Even Onesimus might not have been able to articulate clearly why he would think of Paul. Is it because he wanted to ease the tension with his master? Is it because he wanted to be freed from his bondage as a slave? Is it because he wanted to regain his human dignity? It could have been all of these reasons. No matter what, the core drive must have been related to his hunger to be viewed as a human again after a prolonged experience of being viewed as a tool alone. If you are not living in Roman society, it may not be easy for you to identify with the Romans' instrumental view on slaves. Some of the slaves were well treated and even owned property and their own slaves. Those slaves who served a master with high honor and status in society may hold many resources and even power. One of the reasons is that it was not honorable for people to work. Instead, people with honor were expected to use their minds to understand the universe and the future of the empire. Therefore, the upper class in Roman society used slaves to help them to do business because it was not honorable to do it by themselves.

Chapter 6

FREEDOM IN LOVE

6.1. INTRODUCTION

VALJEAN HAS NO WORLDLY obligation to Cosette nor to Fantine. He takes up the responsibility of raising Cosette because of love, not worldly obligation. He understands Fantine's situation because he has had similar experiences and had been transformed by the bishop's love. He knows how it feels to be abandoned, and to have the power to love. He therefore takes Cosette as his own daughter and raises her at all costs. This is the transformative power of love. It turns a man full of hatred into one full of love. It transforms the bad experiences into the experiences that help one to understand others.

Valjean devoted his whole life to protecting and nurturing Cosette. They grow together and run away together. They become a genuine family and establish a true bond of love. Cosette was no longer a burden to Valjean, but his treasure. Fantine did not leave him a problem to solve but a mission to complete. Through the process of raising Cosette, Valjean found his value and humanity again. To love is not only to give but to nurture and realize one's own created value. However, we need someone to love. That is why the Bible tells us to love our neighbors as ourselves. It is through loving our neighbors that we can experience our loving nature and power. It is Cosette who transforms Valjean further into someone who is deeply caring and loving.

With such a deep bonding, there came the biggest challenge for Valjean. He received a letter written by Marius to say goodbye to Cosette, showing that they both loved each another, because he was planning to die for his higher calling. Valjean knew clearly that Marius was in great danger because he was at the barricade. This posed a dilemma for Valjean, because if Marius were to die, Cosette could stay with him. However, if he saved Marius, he would lose Cosette, because as a runaway criminal, he knows he cannot stay with them. How will love be shown in this situation? Keep Cosette, the one you love, with you, or let her go free to be in love with whoever she loves? Valjean loved her so much he let her free.

It is love that set Valjean free. It is also love that gave Valjean the power to let Cosette love freely. The power of love will spread and have a great impact. Valjean was set free by the bishop's love. He knows well the power of love and the purpose of freedom. The freedom granted by the bishop has a purpose and he has achieved it.

6.2. INNER TEXTURE: LOVE IN FREEDOM; FREEDOM TO LOVE

> I am sending him, that is, my own heart, back to you. I wanted to keep him with me, so that he might be of service to me in your place during my imprisonment for the gospel; but I preferred to do nothing without your consent, in order that your good deed might be voluntary and not something forced.

PHILEMON 12–14

Having introduced Onesimus's new identity and relationship with Paul and Philemon, Paul rhetorically says he is now sending him back to the household of Philemon. What? Send a slave back to his master and call that love? This act is anticlimactic. Readers including Philemon and you may have expected that Paul will ask Philemon to free Onesimus because he has the right and the authority as well as so many reasons to do so. But he didn't, and even more unexpectedly, he choose to send Onesimus back to Philemon's household. Sending him back has two theologically and rhetorically important implications. Theologically, freedom is the result of God's salvation. In Gal 5:1, Paul says, "For freedom Christ has set us free. Stand firm, therefore, and do not submit again to a yoke of slavery." So we have to try our very best not to be controlled by contemporary values again but to live a life that is worthy of the gospel. To Philemon, this could have meant forgoing exercising his power as a slave master and respecting Onesimus's freedom. Paul should not only have taught Philemon about the importance of the gospel but also about the freedom the gospel will bring to him. The rhetorical effect of Paul's own example of respecting Philemon's freedom and his wording expecting Philemon's good deed to be voluntary and not something forced is demonstrating what obedience to faith is. You obey wholeheartedly what you believe to be true and right.

In v. 12, Paul further describes Onesimus as τὰ ἐμὰ σπλάγχνα (ta ema splaychna), "my own heart." This articulation of Onesimus actually picks up the line of argument in vv. 10–11 trying to remind Philemon Onesimus is not property nor a thing but a human being who can be loved. So Paul actually escalates his articulation of the intensity of his relationship with Onesimus by using the Greek word σπλάγχνα, which literally means one's deep compassion. It is the same word used in the Synoptic Gospels to describe Jesus' compassion when he sees those who are lost (Matt 9:36; 14:14; Mark 6:34) and the reaction of the good Samaritan who sees his neighbor (Luke 10:33). This is a word referring to one's deep self. So saying that Onesimus is his own σπλάγχνα is much stronger than merely saying that he is his son. This escalation is part of Paul's rhetoric that builds through the whole letter until vv. 15–16 where Paul explicitly states his request. The gap between the prevailing attitudes toward a slave and the Christian brotherhood relationship is so great that it will not have been realistic for Paul to voice his request without any psychological or rhetorical preparation. From "my child" to "my heart," the intensity has increased and the closeness to Paul has been increased.

Verses 12–13 actually repeat the same theme of vv. 8–9. The meaning of v. 13 is very dense stating at least four justified reasons to keep Onesimus with Paul. First, Paul's wish surely counts and he restates that he wants to keep Onesimus for the right purpose. In order to emphasize it is Paul's wish, he adds ἐγώ (*ego*), meaning I, in front of βουλόμην (*bouloman*), meaning I wish, which has already contained the meaning of "I." Secondly, Paul explains that the purpose of keeping Onesimus is not for Paul's own good but to serve the gospel. Thirdly, Paul reminds Philemon that, originally, this is his duty to do so. These three reasons are strong and persuasive enough. Everyone expects Paul to use this power to ask Philemon to let Onesimus stay with him. Paul rhetorically says he chooses to let Philemon do the good deed based on his own free will. What is the rhetorical purpose of this choice? This is not just a saying but an action. What is the effect of Paul's model then? This action actually echoes two of Paul's important theological thoughts, freedom in Christ and modeling ("Be imitators of me, as I am of Christ," 1 Cor 11:1), which will be explored in the next section.

6.3. INTERTEXTUAL TEXTURE: FREEDOM AND MODELING IN PAUL

It is hard for us to understand why Paul has to use such a complicated way to persuade Philemon. One of the reasons is we have not grasped how important freedom is to Paul. Freedom to Paul is not the freedom we understand in a capitalist society which means mainly our unboundedness to make our own choices. It is the core value of salvation. With the eschatological perspective, introduced in chapter 5, in mind, a new life in Christ brings two gifts. On the one hand, we are still living in this sinful age with different kinds of lies, distorted values, and relationships. These distorted values will bring broken relationships and hurt into our lives. We cannot deny that we are wounded and hurting. We must have had different experiences of being hurt by people who hold these distorted values or by the unfair social system itself. However, we may also be the one who has hurt another for we cannot be isolated from these prevailing values and not be affected by them. In order to be a new creation in Christ, we are set free from these two old aspects. We are free from our own hurts and we are free from being in bondage to these values.

The world translated as "freedom" in Greek is ἐλεύθερος (eleutheros). It was used in Greek culture to refer to a state in contrast with slavery. Slavery means someone is being subjugated by another. ἐλεύθερος refers to a state that is free from another's control. In addition, in politics, it usually refers to people who are under self-government but are not governed.[1] This sense of "freedom from" also appears in Paul's theological thoughts, but is used in a deeper sense. It is not only freedom from external coercion, but also inner sinful drives. Therefore, we can see Paul says "free from the bondage of decay" in Rom 8:21, "freedom from sin" in Rom 6:18–23, and "freedom from the law" in Rom 7:3; 8:2; and Gal 2:4. The word translated as bondage actually comes from the same root word as slave. This view is different from the Stoic view of freedom which assumes a man can control himself to be free from external control. Paul acknowledges that we are not free in our inner selves because we are still living in this sinful world. We need God's grace to set us free from these bondages and hurts.

To Philemon, this bondage of decay may refer to the values he adopted as a slave master. Seeing a slave not as a man created by God but as property, exploiting his productivity without caring about his well-being, and treating him merely as a tool are all values of decay. The worst of all is they may perceive that as being reasonable according to the prevailing values. Those slaves, such as Onesimus, would be deeply hurt. Being a captured slave, or born as a slave, they were hurt everyday physically or psychologically. How can a slave be healed? Similarly, we who live in this capitalist society may also be indoctrinated with many capitalist values. We may believe that "private" property rights provide the core

1. Schlier, *TDNT*, 287–490.

54

momentum for a society to grow and therefore we may refuse to share our "private" property with the poor. We may also believe that a free market is fair and therefore poor people are just less competitive and do not require our sympathy at all. People are being hurt unawares. Those who are losers in a capitalist society may believe this loser identity themselves and not be aware of the unfairness of the rules behind the game. These values and wounds are not external coercion but are beliefs with which we have been indoctrinated. We have to be freed from these values, distorted identities, or wounds that hold us in bondage to decay.

More important, salvation is not merely about "freedom from" but "freedom to." We have new meaning in our lives. Freedom from is about restoration and freedom to is about recreation. As Christians, we are not only passively freed from the bondage of this age, but become agents to live out our heavenly values freely. This can be clearly seen in Gal 5: 13–14, "For you were called to freedom, brothers and sisters; only do not use your freedom as an opportunity for self-indulgence, but through love become slaves to one another. For the whole law is summed up in a single commandment, 'You shall love your neighbor as yourself.'" In v. 13, Paul reminds us that we are all called to freedom. However, such freedom is eschatological, which means it can be expressed in this world but does not belong to this world. We are free from the bondage of this world but still have to be aware of the temptations of this world. Our freedom has a purpose, and that is to exercise love in all we do.

In v. 13b, Paul reminds us that this freedom has to be expressed through love as we become slaves to one another. That verse echoes v. 1 in the same chapter where Paul just warns the Galatians not to resubmit themselves to the yoke of slavery. He uses an imperative form of the verb δουλεύω (douleuo), which originated from δοῦλος (doulos), meaning "slave," and can mean to be a slave of someone, to state the true purpose of our freedom. Our freedom should not be used to re-enslave ourselves, and we should not use the freedom to satisfy our own desires either. Instead, we should be a slave to others. Jesus has demonstrated

55

this model of slavery to us. In Phil 2:6–7, Paul articulates Jesus as "though he was in the form of God, did not regard equality with God as something to be exploited, but emptied himself, taking the form of a slave, being born in human likeness. And being found in human form." In here, Jesus also exercises his freedom to forgo his godliness and take the form of a slave to serve us.

6.4. NARRATIVE FIVE: JOURNEY OF SOUL SEARCHING

Onesimus knew clearly that he had to leave Philemon's household. That said, he did not really know where to go. He wanted to find Paul, but he did not know where exactly he was. This journey was a journey to search for Paul, but it was also a search for his own soul. He didn't know whether he would be back or was leaving forever, so he wrote a letter telling Philemon that he was trying to find Paul in the hopes that he could help him to solve his inner struggle and do better at his job. Trying not to catch others' attention, he only packed a few personal belongings, along with the *peculium* he had saved over the past few years.

Peculium is a Latin word that literally means "private property," it refers sometimes to a slave's private savings. You may wonder how a slave can own anything when he himself is the property of others. Yes, legally speaking, slaves were allowed to use these savings, but this *peculium* still also belonged to the master. This policy was entirely for management's sake. In order to maintain the motivation of slaves, the Roman slavery system used both a carrot and a stick. *Peculium* is part of the carrot. First, the slavery system was sustained by the ultimate hope of freedom. Therefore, Roman slavery had a very clear policy on manumission, with various degrees involved. In order to be manumitted, slaves had to gain their master's trust and love. Moreover, even if the master finally decided to free his slaves, the slaves had to save enough money to pay for their own freedom. Their master would pay little tips or award some pocket money to a slave who did a satisfactory job for them, which is why a slave would have a *peculium*. It was a very smart way to manage slaves, as no one had enough time to monitor every move of a slave. Giving them a long-term hope together with a short-term reward kept slaves loyal and efficient even when no one was overseeing them.

There was a full moon the night Onesimus left Philemon's household. Although the future was not certain, Onesimus already felt the difference. It was the first time since he had started to work in Philemon's household that he did not go out this door to serve others' purposes. He had nearly forgotten the feeling of living for himself. He was the one who would decide where he would go, who he would visit, and the purpose of his life. The feeling was so strange, but invigorating. He walked slowly under the full moonlight, trying to feel more deeply that rare feeling of genuine existence. He was alone, but he did not feel lonely that night.

After a whole night of walking, he finally reached another nearby town. He walked into the market without any order to fulfill. He bought freshly baked bread from one of the stores. The owner could tell Onesimus was a slave, so he asked whether his household needed more. Slaves seldom bought one piece of bread because urban households usually had a large number of household members. Onesimus replied with a smile, "No, I bought this bread for myself." The smile was not merely for the bread but also for the "self." Words cannot explain how happy Onesimus was at the moment he realized once again that he was a genuine person and not an instrument. He could buy something and eat it for himself. However, this happiness did not stay too long before it was replaced by fear and puzzlement. He was afraid when he realized that he might have to return to Philemon's house, bear punishment, or have nowhere to go. In Roman society, working individually without a household or a patron was nearly impossible. Many runaway slaves became bandits simply because they had no other alternative. He was at a loss because he had been living like an instrument and had been seen as an instrument.

Chapter 7

RELATIONSHIP RESTORATION

7.1. INTRODUCTION

SOCIETY IS FULL OF DIVISIONS. Rich and poor, noble and pleb, honor and dishonor, powerful and powerless, master and slave, black and white, and many more dividing lines in our societies, both ancient and modern. These dividing lines, though invisible, penetrate every part of our daily lives. You cannot see these lines but you can surely see the result of them or the things that demarcate them. In Roman society, only Roman citizens could wear a toga, which marked the special status and rights of Romans. In the nineteenth century, the beginning of industrialization, the gap between rich and poor was so wide that you could not only see it but smell it, because those poor people could only live in an area surrounded with rats and rubbish. They lived in such places just because they could not afford to live somewhere else. However, this gap was not necessary nor justified.

The barricade in the novel is symbolic. It clearly separates the soldiers from those revolutionaries. However, it is more than that. It separates the suppressed from the suppressor. It separates those who have power and guns from those who have dreams. It separates those who care about others from those who only follow orders. It separates those who are bonded to mission with those who are bonded to the power hierarchy. Having said that, we can see genuine brotherhood inside the barricade. Although most of those revolutionaries were poor (though some did come from the upper class), they joined and led the revolution because they believed in justice and still had a dream for a better country. They were not fighting for themselves. They resisted because of love. They loved their neighbors and those who had no blood relationship with them. Although they were living in the upper class, they could see the suffering of the poor.

There is a very touching scene in the movie *Les Misérables*. When Marius is giving his speech in the forum encouraging the people to join the movement, he is noticed by one of his family members. He is scolded, "Do you know what you just did has made your family ashamed." Yes, according to the prevailing values, Marius should do what other noble class members do and avoid doing anything that could infringe upon the honor and privileged rights of his family. He has no need to do anything for the poor or sacrifice his honor and bear the corresponding cost. He might lose the respect of his family members and all the benefits of being a member of a noble family. What he does is not because of external forces but from within. He sees the poor's desperate situation. He sees the corruption of the system. He sees his mission.

It is this "seeing" and his sense of mission that call him to cross those social barricades and build a physical barricade to defend his mission and call. It is this higher call that gives him the power to break all social dividing lines to form a genuine brotherhood with those coming from different social status. This brotherhood surpasses all existing social relationships at that moment of time. They come together not through a motive of self-interest, but because they dream together, support each other, and bear each other. The calling breaks all walls and barricades and restores genuine relationships.

7.2. INNER TEXTURE: EXHORTATION OF BROTHERHOOD RELATIONSHIP

> Perhaps this is the reason he was separated from you for a while, so that you might have him back forever, no longer as a slave but more than a slave, a beloved brother—especially to me but how much more to you, both in the flesh and in the Lord.

> PHILEMON 15–16

Having paved the way rhetorically for forteen verses, Paul finally voices his ultimate request for Onesimus. If we do not hold to the runaway slave hypothesis, it would not be too difficult to hear Paul's request in vv. 15–17. Elevating Onesimus's identity from Paul's Child to his heart, it is time to voice the ultimate relationship that Paul wants to restore between Philemon and Onesimus. Again, this ultimate request is theologically and rhetorically packed together. Paul does not only aim at a worldly release of Onesimus, but a transformation of Philemon, and his relationship with Onesimus. As said in a previous chapter, if Paul merely wanted Philemon to manumit Onesimus because he was useful to Paul or had a good relationship with Paul, he could simply use his power to order Philemon to do what was right. However, this move would still be following the instrumental values the world places on a human being. Paul does not choose to do so, but uses all kinds of rhetorical tools and theological reasoning to persuade Philemon because he aims at restoration of a relationship which can only be achieved through love and in one's free will.

Paul's request in vv. 15–17 focuses on Onesimus but also on Philemon. Paul wishes that his letter will remind Philemon of what he may have taught Philemon while he was previously staying with Philemon. He wants Philemon to be able to choose to restore Onesimus's relationship out of his own transformation, love, and free will. Therefore, Paul carefully crafted the letter addressing every distortion in the value of, and relationship with, Onesimus. And then comes the final request.

In v. 15, Paul first provides the reason for the whole incident, including the departure of Onesimus, his meeting with Paul, and his returning to Philemon. Paul uses a Greek preposition, δια (*dia*), followed by an accusative pronoun usually referring to a reason. Paul here proposes that Philemon was separated from Onesimus for a while so that he may receive or have him forever. There are actually two reasons that are suggested. First, it is rather implicit. The verb separated was used in the passive voice, athough Onesimus was obviously leaving by his own will. This kind of passive voice was called the divine passive and conveyed a message that God is in control.[1] (Though we are doing things actively they are in his plan. Greek writers used a passive form to indicate God's reign.) So, Paul is actually reminding Philemon that, no matter what the actual cause of Onesimus's leaving was, it is in God's plan and under God's sovereignty. This implies that Onesimus's new identity and new relationship in Christ are under God's reign also.

Besides the reminder that God is in control, Paul further strengthens his argument suggesting that the short (ὥραν; *horan*) separation may lead to an eternal (αἰώνιον; *aionion*) relationship. It is the first time Paul directly mentions Onesimus's eternal relationship with Philemon. In the first fourteen verses, Paul mainly articulates his relationship with Onesimus in preparing Philemon to accept his new relationship with Onesimus. In introducing this eternal relationship, Paul suggests that it is because of God's plan to emphasize the theological reason behind it. It is not only for persuasion's sake but it is also Paul's true belief.

Unlike the English translation, which separates it into two separate sentences, vv. 15 and 16 are one complete sentence in the Greek. The ending of v. 15 concerning the eternal relationship is just the beginning of Paul's request. He then turns to Onesimus's worldly relationship. He is now no longer "as" a slave but more than a slave. That is a clear request. In the eternal relationship, Onesimus is no longer a slave. This is the only verse in which Paul mentions slave. However, he does not say Onesimus is a slave, but adds a Greek word, ὡς (*hos*), "as," before the word "slave." Scholars

1. Fitzmyer, *Philemon*, 112.

suggest this may reflect Paul's refusal to recognize the slavery system so that he does not dare to call Onesimus a slave.[2] Even when he has to mention the slavery system, he added ὡς to show his disapproval of the institution. This is consistent with Paul's eschatological perspective that, on the one hand, although we are still living in this world, we do not necessarily follow and agree with its values and institutions. On the other hand, we have to follow the heavenly values that include seeing each other as brothers in Christ.

How far is the distance between a slave and a brother? We may not be able to use any definite number to measure the distance. To Paul, it is far enough that Paul used a great deal of effort to design every single piece of rhetoric in the letter to bring Philemon out of his prevailing values and attitudes toward a slave and remind him of the heavenly values we have received from Christ. In order to distinguish this brotherhood from the ordinary type of fraternity treasured by the Romans, Paul added "beloved" in front of "brother" and states clearly that this brotherhood is not only in the flesh but also in Christ. To accept a slave as a brother in Christ is much more than just manumission in the flesh. To accept someone as a brother implies that we have to transcend social values and prejudices. This is a more demanding request, requiring Philemon's heartfelt response rather than merely following an order from someone with authority.

7.3. INTERTEXTUAL TEXTURE: BROTHERHOOD IN CHRIST

What is so special about being called brother and sister by members of the believing community? Sometimes, we forget the essence of that relationship and how hard it can be to have a genuine brotherhood relationship. We are living in a world filled with different kinds of walls separating us from each other. These walls are so real that we cannot see people on the other side of the walls as

---

2. Callahan, "Paul's Epistle to Philemon," 371.

human beings, let alone loving them. We need God's love so we can break through these walls and be loving again. That is why we are called a new creation. Having God's love, we are healed and freed from the old bondages. Most important of all, we can be loving again. This loving identity has to be practiced and is most relevant to the group of people who are following and belonging to Jesus. This community has the mission of loving one another or loving their neighbors as themselves. This loving nature becomes their identity. But how can we comprehend this loving nature with the walls separating us.

That is exactly why we are called brothers and sisters (ἀδελφοί; *adelphoi*). In Rom 14:15, Paul says, "If your brother or sister is being injured by what you eat, you are no longer walking in love." Loving each other becomes the qualifying essence of brothers and sisters. The direct instruction for that kind of brotherly love is found in Rom 12:10a: "Love one another with mutual affection." Paul here uses two similar but complementing words, φιλαδελφία (*philadelphia*) and φιλόςτοργος (*phlostorgos*), to emphasize the transcendent family relationship among members of the believing community. On the one hand, the word translated as love, φιλαδελφία, that is used to distinguish what Paul wants to refer to here is different from the αγάπη also translated as love. φιλαδελφία is composed from φιλός and αδελφός in which φιλός (*philos*) means basically love among friends, and αδελφός can mean brother (and sister) and is quite often used to refer to members of religious associations. So φιλαδελφία is used here to refer to love among members of religious associations.[3] The Greek word φιλόςτοργος, translated as "mutual affection" in the NRSV, refers to love for a family member. James Dunn is right to articulate Paul's use of these two words as "part of the redefinition of boundaries in which Paul engages—a sense of family belongingness which transcended immediate family ties and did not depend on natural or ethnic bonds."[4]

---

3. Dunn, *Romans*, 740.
4. Dunn, *Romans*, 741.

It is true historically and in reality that we can be blood siblings or called brother and sister in church but lack any genuine affection and love toward each other. The reason is mainly due to the invisible walls among us. The underlying social values and identities are part of the cause. In NT times, honor and shame were the most influential social values. It determined people's view of others. Some people were more highly honored and some were less, or even shamed. And the social value system drove people to get together with people of higher honor and distance themselves from people who had been shamed because your honor in the eyes of other people was affected by the people associated with you. Moreover, as people believed that honor is fixed in quantity, in order to get higher honor, they competed for it and therefore rivalry was a necessary consequence. It is within this context that Paul says in Rom 12:10b, "Outdo one another in showing honor." Instead of following the way people strive for their own honor and to accumulate their own honor, Paul reminds the congregation in Romans to do things in a different way and shows them how it should be done.

Romans 12:16 echoes how it should be done in reality. Paul says, "Live in harmony with one another; do not be haughty, but associate with the lowly; do not claim to be wiser than you are." In the Greek, Paul uses the word φρονοῦντες (*thronountes*), usually translated as "mind." Dunn suggests that Paul asks the congregation to have the same mind or same attitude on a deeper level of their lives.[5] Fitzmyer suggests that Paul hopes they would have the same regard for each other.[6] This reminder would surely have been effective even in Roman society where diversity regarding the value of honor and social status was common. That could also be the reason why Paul strengthened his view further by saying that one should not think too highly of oneself and be willing to associate with the lowly. This use of "high" and "low" clearly implies the existence of diversity among the communities. It could be ethnic diversity, including Jews and Greeks, and social diversities,

---

5. Dunn, *Romans*, 747.

6. Fitzmyer, *Romans*, 656.

including rich and poor, slave and free, patron and client, in the community. To Paul, every person being a brother of each other implies the acceptance of the transcending value of love, and giving up following the prevailing values, and therefore brotherhood is not only nominal but has real essence. It is not only an obligation to fulfill but a gift to taste. We have to practice these implied values and powers so as to experience the reality of the eschatological creation. It is an identity reflected in our daily lives which is linked to eternal life. It is an eschatological reality as it reminds us of our heavenly identity of loving others when we are still living in this world full of walls established by our diversity of ethnic origin, economic status, social status, and a diversity in perceptions of honor. Therefore, reminding Philemon to accept Onesimus as a beloved brother is to remind him of his own heavenly identity.

The same message is also true for us who live in the twenty-first century. There are walls separating us from God, from other people, and from ourselves. There are new and old walls. Some come from the giant, Capitalism. Some from high technology, like big data and the social media originally promised to connect us. The appearance of social media like Facebook promised to help people become more connected to each other. Yes, but no. The outcome is polarized. We surely have moments of feeling more connected, but we are also more divided. The mode of social media habituates us to view the world from the perspective of apparent facts, rather than from looking into details. This makes it easier for people to be manipulated by fake news and manmade labeling. Hatred can be created more easily by a selected view of photos and sometimes by edited video.

As a Christian, we cannot escape from these walls. More importantly, we are called to live out our calling in this broken world. That is the reason why Jesus had to come to this world and became flesh among us to experience all these tensions. Most important of all, he wants to demonstrate to us how reconciliation can be accomplished through love. He does not only provide an example but also calls us to follow him to be the agents of reconciliation.

Reconciliation is not only a theological concept but also a gift and a mission for our daily lives.

7.4. NARRATIVE SIX: ENCOUNTERING PAUL; ENCOUNTERING LOVE

It did not take too long to find out that Paul was in custody in Ephesus. His charge was disturbing the peace of the Roman Empire. The arrest had nothing to do with religion; the Roman Empire was very inclusive of religious perspectives. However, they were very sensitive to opportunities for riots or other forms of turmoil that could affect the image of the Pax Romana that the empire had tried very hard to build up. Paul was famous among Jews, but not in good way. He was controversial, and he brought arguments everywhere he stayed. He was a Jew himself, but he taught the story of another Jew who made many Jewish leaders very angry. He also went into nearly every Jewish synagogue of each city he visited to share his special perspective about that controversial Jew called Jesus. Although it took several days of walking to find Paul, Onesimus was determined to do so.

Having found Paul in Ephesus, Onesimus was allowed to visit him because of the privilege given to Paul's Roman citizen status. Onesimus had very mixed feelings. On the one hand, he was happy because he had finally found Paul and was allowed to talk to him. On the other, he was also worried because he was not sure whether Paul would recognize him or how he should introduce himself and his situation. It was totally unexpected to Onesimus that Paul did not only recognize him but also knew why he had come such a long way to him.

"Come, my son, Onesimus. You must be very tired and hungry after such a long journey. You can stay here with me as long as I am not being sent somewhere else." Paul seemed to know that Onesimus had nowhere to go or stay. They did not talk much that day. Paul was busy with others, writing letters with some and meeting with others. It was rare in the Roman Empire to address people who had no blood relationship with you as your brother and sister. Sitting next to Paul, Onesimus heard what Paul taught those visitors and the messages in those letters he wrote. These messages were new to Onesimus, and for some reason they were very attractive to him. His heart filled and he began to think that he would like to know more about the Jesus that Paul always mentioned.

"Master, may I hear more about the Jesus you always mention? Who is he? Why would someone who died on the cross be praised? Shouldn't it be shameful to be nailed to the cross?" Onesimus used all his bravery to ask.

"Don't call me master. We have only one Lord: Jesus, whom you want to know more about. He is God, but he chose to come in human form to serve us. You may not believe that I once persecuted followers of him wholeheartedly. However, this Jesus revealed himself to me directly and called me to preach him to all the nations. After I met him directly, I could not resist his call because I had not experienced such fulfillment in my heart before. I try very hard to live a life that conforms to those traditions that promise to bring us closer to God and separates us from this sinful world. However, I cannot find the same fulfillment I had when I met Jesus. He told me who I am and my value of living. I suddenly understand my value in him. I was a new creation, free from my previous bondage and called to live a new life to serve this world with Jesus as a model." Onesimus was very attracted to Paul's gentle speech. He could not understand why others called Paul a rioter. He was only preaching about a man who had come to serve them. It may be that to serve others and not to be served truly endangered one of the core values in the Roman Empire: self-seeking. Because of the nature of honor and shame, people competed to acquire higher honor and, at the same time, had to show off their honor, as it was confirmed by being seen by others. In that sense, Jesus' gentleness was subversive, as was his self-sacrificing love, *agape*.

Chapter 8

GENUINE FELLOWSHIP
Bearing One Another

8.1. INTRODUCTION

ONE OF THE MOST touching and impressive points concerning *Les Misérables* is the connectedness of the different characters. They come from different backgrounds and were originally not related to each other. However, they become connected with each other tightly through the ripple effect of the bishop's loving action toward Valjean. Valjean did steal the precious silver, but the bishop considers them to be gifts to Valjean. This loving action of bearing another's burden transformed Valjean so that he gave up his hatred and became a man of love. He not only became a good businessman and mayor but also a man willing to bear others' burdens, most important of all, Fantine's final wish. Valjean's example of bearing one another's burdens was not only inherited by Cosette, but also by her husband. His life was lifted by a genuine loving act and it becomes a light to light up others. This mutual bearing-of-burdens relationship is the key characteristic of a genuine fellowship.

The bond of a genuine fellowship does not depend on whether the members belong to the same social class nor on their economic value, but on whether they have the same mission and willingness to bear one another's burdens. Those who stayed within the barricade were part of a genuine fellowship because they fought for the same mission and were willing to support one another. The little boy Gavroche was kind to everyone even under the very unfavorable conditions of poverty and injustice. He shared their mission and was brave enough to become part of the barricade fellowship. His death definitely brings hurt to the fellowship, but also creates a great contrast between the bonding within the barricade and the cold bloodiness outside it.

Bearing one another's burdens is not only giving, it is also receiving. Valjean received the greatest gift of his life through raising Cosette. The janitor in the monastery who helps them to hide from the police is the one Valjean saved on the street by pulling away the heavy wooden pillar pressed on his body. Our greatest gift sometimes may not be the things we strive for but a chance to use who we are to serve someone in need. When we use ourselves to bear another's burdens, it actualizes our potential and created values. The values of our societies, both ancient and modern, drive us to follow the values of this world, which so emphasize owning and consuming, and to forget our own mission and created values. Self-interest, instrumental values, and consumerism are common fake values that mislead our lives. Self-interest isolates us from others. Instrumental values blind us from seeing others as genuine people with value. Consumerism makes us forget we have a mission to fulfill, and the greatest happiness is to be found in fulfilling our mission.

Genuine fellowship is the form of connection which is totally Christ based and Christ fueled. It is also countercultural. It represents the form of Christian existence that genuinely follows Christ, who came to reconcile but not separate, who values every one of us and frees us from bondage so that we can fulfill our new mission. To call someone to be in a fellowship is not just to call them to come and share shallow things, but to call them to enter a new countercultural existence that shares the same mission and bears each other's burdens.

8.2. INNER TEXTURE: WELCOMING ONESIMUS AS PAUL

> So if you consider me your partner [i.e., fellowship], welcome him as you would welcome me. If he has wronged you in any way, or owes you anything, charge that to my account. I, Paul, am writing this with my own hand: I will repay it. I say nothing about your owing me even your own self.
>
> PHILEMON 17–19

What if Philemon has been successfully persuaded by Paul? In what ways is Onesimus received as a brother when he is still a slave? Or he is still struggling with the practical issues, including the problems with receiving a slave into a household and the consequences of taking a slave as a brother in a household, after following the advice of Paul? Does that imply Philemon has to manumit Onesimus? Is it possible? As there must have been other slaves in Philemon's household, it would have been very costly for Philemon to manumit Onesimus because it will have some implications regarding his other slaves. Paul seems to have expected these struggles and addressed them in his rhetorical argument.

Following up on his ultimate request in v. 16, Paul uses his own relationship with Philemon as the grounds on which to answer the possible questions in Philemon's mind. Paul mentions again the concept of κοινωνός (koinōnos), meaning partner, fellowship or sharing, as their form of relationship. Sara Winter suggests that Paul uses this concept in a similar way to the Latin term societa, referring mainly to a common form of business partnership in the first century.[1] Paul Sampley, who thoroughly researched the concept of societa, suggests that societa is not a concrete form of partnership requiring the signing of a contract or other details. Instead, it only requires a common agreement about entering into a project or works with the same purpose, sometimes concluded with a hand shake.[2] So when Paul says, "If you consider me your

1. Winter, "Methodological Observations," 11–12.

2. Sampley, *Pauline Partnership*, 79.

κοινωνόν [partner]," he could have been making use of the terms' business as well as theological essence to remind Philemon. On the one hand, from the perspective of the business use, it could mean they have a similar working purpose, which refers to preaching the gospel. On the other hand, from theological perspective, it could mean they share the same mission and are entering into a deep relationship with Christ. The most likely explanation for Paul's use of κοινωνός is to make use of its key essences in both senses, including its close ties to a relationship with a similar goal, and the mutual burden-bearing nature of the relationship.

Paul then asks Philemon to προσλαβοῦ ὡς ἐμέ (*proslabou hos mem*), meaning "receive or welcome someone as me." This reception is based on taking Paul as their partner, meaning doing so with the same vision and will, bearing with one another. That is to say, Paul asks Philemon to take Onesimus as one with the same mission as Paul and bear his burdens as he would do for Paul. This again is counter to Roman culture. Everyone is trying to sit with and be friends with those who are more honored. No highly honored Roman would place himself equal to another person with less honor because this would actually be detrimental to one's own honor.[3] However, this is exactly what Jesus has done for us and what Paul wanted to demonstrate to Philemon as an example again. The rhetorical effect of asking Philemon to receive Onesimus as he would Paul the partner is that it sets the ground as well as provides room and flexibility for Philemon to design how exactly Onesimus is to be received. This flexibility is necessary because Philemon was still living under the Roman Empire. He was still subject to Roman law and other institutions associated with Roman slavery. The sad fact was that manumission was not a simple solution. On the one hand, a manumitted slave can still work under his former master, but just in a different relationship as a client. If the master was not satisfied with their performance or services, he could re-enslave the manumitted slave. That means if the master has not genuinely transformed the relationship, the exploitative nature will not be changed. On the other hand, the

3. Ip, *Socio-Rhetorical Interpretation*, 91–92.

Roman economy was not like the contemporary economy in which one can start up one's own business. Social relationships in the Roman economy were highly connected and dependent. Those who had no power had to depend on their patron or master to provide job opportunities. Separating oneself from this hierarchy was not realistic.

Verse 18 picks up the practical concerns Philemon may have had in mind when considering taking Onesimus as his brother. Peter O'Brien explains that this conditional sentence has two possible meanings. First, it could be hypothetical in form but referring to an actual offence Onesimus has committed against Philemon. If one follows the runaway hypothesis, the reason will be logical. The next explanation provided is that the conditional sentence is really referring to a financial cost resulting from Onesimus's absence.[4] I think the second scenario is more reasonable. However, I suggest that the financial cost for the genuine transformation of the relationship may be more than that resulting from Onesimus's absence. It should not be very difficult to understand that accepting a slave as a brother will mean exploiting him will no longer be an option. Philemon may still maintain Onesimus's social status as a slave, but he can no longer do the same things that may have been taken for granted before, to this brother. This brotherly slave relationship must therefore embody the opportunity to incur a cost in productivity and maybe efficiency.

The key point here actually is not what the possible cost Philemon may have incurred was, but Paul's example as demonstrated here. He once again promised to bear the cost. Bearing another's burden is the key essence of a κοινωνός.[5] Therefore, the theme of the whole section is clear. In v. 17, Paul begs Philemon to receive Onesimus as he would Paul himself. There must have been a cost involved when Philemon forwent the right to exploit a slave. The final sentence reminds Philemon that Paul also bears the cost for him.

4. O'Brien, *Colossians, Philemon*, 299.

5. Ip, *Socio-Rhetorical Interpretation*, 43.

8.3. INTERTEXTUAL TEXTURE: PAUL'S VIEW OF COMMUNITY

It may not be hard for us to understand what Paul says but it will be very difficult for us to feel Paul's urge to receive Onesimus as a brother and as a partner. The main reason for that is also the underlying problem addressed by Paul. We, that is Philemon and us, may be affected by the prevailing values surrounding us. It was Roman values for Philemon and capitalist values for us. Living in the twenty-first century, we are born and raised in a society that upholds individualistic values and emphasizes the importance of privateness. We may misunderstand that our new life in Christ is also a renewal in an individual only. We may forget the communal nature of our new life. It would not have been easy for Philemon also, having lived for so long as a slave master and influenced by the Roman values, to accept a slave as his partner and brother. That is the reason Paul uses so much rhetoric to remind and persuade Philemon to take off his colored glasses.

Along Paul's theological lines of thought, this countercultural togetherness is an essential quality for the new creation. In this age, Christians sometimes take the concept of a new creation in too abstract a way, and overlook Paul's concern for its practical form. Of course, when we talk about the practical form of a heavenly value, it has eschatological nature. In order to understand Paul's teaching on community, we will examine Paul's use of the word ἐκκλησία (ekklesia), usually translated as the church, and his use of the family metaphor for members of the church. Understanding the deeper sense of these communal concepts can illuminate our understanding concerning the essence of being that forms escha-tological reality: the new creation.

The eschatological nature of ἐκκλησία. The basic meaning of the word ἐκκλησία is "call out" and refers to "assembly" in the Hebrew Bible, and Roman people with voting rights gathering to discuss policy. ἐκκλησία is usually translated as "church." Schol-ars have debated whether "call out" or "assembly" is more likely to be the meaning the NT writers wanted to convey. I think it is not necessarily an either-or situation but could be both. That is to say, the church can refer to those people called out as an assembly.[6] They gather because they have the same mission. From that, gathering is the form and calling is the essence. This identity reaches across social and ethic status and is linked to the same call. In that sense, in 1 Cor 1:2, Paul uses, "To the church [ἐκκλησία] of God that is in Corinth, to those who are sanctified in Christ Jesus, called to be saints, together with all those who in every place call on the name of our Lord Jesus Christ, both their Lord and ours": church is an identity referring to those who are sanctified in, called by, and gathered because of Jesus Christ. This is unlike the Roman world where people of the same social status would gather together. For example, those with voting rights will gather in the forum. In 1 Cor 11:18, Paul also refers to the church as those who "come together." When Paul uses ἐκκλησία, he does not refer to those who gather in a specific physical place or with certain rights according to the usage of the word in the Greco-Roman world. Paul uses it, according to Michael Wolter's articulation, to refer to an "assembly for worship that was extraordinary for the everyday world in which it constituted and embodied their identity as a group."[7] It is in that sense of form and essence that Paul addresses the church of God in 2 Cor 1:1; Gal 1:2; 1 Thess 1:1; and Phlm 2.

Unity in Diversity

We are called together because of Christ and in Christ (2 Cor 5:17: "So if anyone is in Christ, there is a new creation"). No matter as an individual Christian or as a church, our identity and calling is anchored in Christ. Christ not only brings us a new identity, but sets an example for us to follow, as Paul says in 1 Cor 11:1, "Be imitators of me, as I am of Christ." His model becomes an ethical direction for us. However, though we have one great model to follow, we are diverse in many aspects. Sociologically, we have different

6. Dunn, *Romans*, 537.

7. Wolter, *Paul*, 260.

socioeconomic statuses. Physically, we are different in our abilities and talents. How can diverse members be one in Christ? Paul knew clearly how high these separating walls were and how hard it could be to break them down. He was once deeply affected by his Jewish beliefs. He saw all Christians as the enemy and a threat to his faith and therefore he persecuted them wholeheartedly. You can sense Paul's great concern about these walls in nearly every one of his letters.

In Rom 12:4–8 and 1 Cor 12:1–30, Paul uses the body metaphor to explain how the plurality of members can be as one in Christ. The oneness is clear in 1 Cor 12:1–11 and 10:17 that we share one bread, receive one spirit, and serve one God. The plurality is also implied in 1 Cor 12:13: "For in one Spirit we were all baptized into one body—Jews or Greeks, slaves or free." The body metaphor does not only deal with the inherent difference among members but also the external distinctions among them.[8] Anthony Thiselton articulated well that the term implies unity in diversity, and diversity in harmony.[9] How could this harmony be achieved? Paul suggested another countercultural view that is mutually needed among members with diverse backgrounds. The membership of a body suggested by Paul is not the same as the membership of other *societa* wherein hierarchy still exists, and the relationships were maintained by making use of others for self-interest purposes. Instead, Paul suggests a belonging and mutually dependent relationship. In 1 Cor 12:15 Paul says 'If the foot were to say, "Because I am not a hand, I do not belong to the body," that would not make it any less a part of the body.' In 1 Cor 12:21–24 Paul specifically addresses the diversity in honor and social status and suggests, on the one hand, that all members are mutually needed. On the other hand, in v. 24 he says God gives greater honor to the inferior member. Paul concludes this solidarity in v. 26 by saying that all members suffer and rejoice together.

It is this mutual-belonging and mutually-needed quality that creates the unity in diversity and gives Christianity its

8. Wolter, *Paul*, 283.

9. Thiselton, *Living Paul*, 103.

distinctiveness. This body metaphor is what Paul had in mind when he asked Philemon to accept Onesimus as his brother and partner. Paul knows that it will not be easy for Philemon, and that is also why he chooses to beg him in love and not give him an order. Love is the foundation of and energy for this unity. Paul explains love right after his body metaphor in Rom 12:9–21 and 1 Cor 13. Love is the reason for all relationship reconciliation. Love helps the loving community to transcend all social prejudice. Love provides the energy for us to bear with each other. Loving each other is the mission for that body. Love is the core value for being a genuine fellowship in which Paul is willing to bear the burden for Onesimus and Philemon, and Paul expects that Philemon will imitate him to bear the burden for Onesimus.

8.4. NARRATIVE SEVEN: FREEDOM AND TRUST

"Please take that letter to Timothy, who was my faithful coworker even when I was in a very difficult time," said Paul. This was a normal task, yet not for a slave. Onesimus was so happy that Paul asked him to help. This request reflected a coworker relationship and a bond of trust. He took the letter and brought it to Timothy's household. This was the not the first time Onesimus had met Timothy, as the man had visited Paul before. However, this was the first time he had the chance to talk to Timothy. "Thanks Onesimus. We are so happy to receive Paul's letter again. We would like to hear Paul's teaching and his recent situation. Is he doing well?" He said "we" because this letter was written to Timothy and his household church. It was normal practice for a letter to be addressed to the head of the household but expected to be heard by the whole household. "Paul is doing well. He is busy with writing and meeting his brothers and sisters who get a chance to come to visit him. I hear a lot about Jesus from him, and I feel very reenergised by his story." Timothy smiled when he heard Onesimus's response, and he said, "The Holy Spirit is starting to work in your heart now, just as he started to work in me. That feeling of energy will keep growing in you, and you will find your new mission and value through walking with faith. Can you help me to take this food to a brother—Festus, meaning joyful—who has been ill for a while? He does not live too far, just on your way back to Paul's house (prison)." Onesimus said, "Yes, master. Oh, sorry. Yes, brother."

Carrying the food on the way back to Paul's house, Onesimus felt very strange again. He had a job to do, but it was not like the work he had needed to do before. He was passionate about this simple task. He could feel energy from inside, and he started to think about how he could help care for this brother. He was not merely doing a job but working on a mission with love. When he arrived at Festus' house, he saw that it was a very humble one, and he could tell it had not been cleaned for a long time. He knocked the door and entered. "Is that Timothy?" The voice was weak but joyful. "I am Onesimus, and I am Timothy's brother." This was the first time Onesimus addressed himself as a brother. "Please come in; I am not able to come greet you." Onesimus then went into the living room and saw that Festus was lying on the bed. Festus was very happy to see Onesimus, making every effort to sit up and introduce himself. Festus was a former slave that had been freed by his master. However, he was not happy even when he was freed because he was poor and still living like a slave. Everything changed after he met Timothy, who introduced Jesus to him by saying what Jesus did for him. He started to do what Jesus did. He was not living for himself but to serve others, and he found his own value in serving his neighbor wholeheartedly. After hearing Festus' story, Onesimus started to help clean his house. Cleaning the house was one of the jobs Onesimus used to do in Philemon's household, but he never experienced a moment of the happiness he did this time, even doing the same job. It was a satisfaction from within. It was work done out of love and freedom, and it had a new value for Onesimus.

On the way back to Paul's house, he remembered what Timothy had told him about the "Holy Spirit." He thought he had really experienced the Holy Spirit through the process of working for Festus. He could not wait to tell Paul what he had experienced today. After hearing Onesimus's story, Paul said, "I am happy to hear that you can feel the Holy Spirit working in you. The Holy Spirit will teach you how to live out a faithful and joyful life himself. I would very much like to keep you here to work for the gospel with me. I enjoy fellowship with you. But I think it's the time for you to go back to Philemon's house. I will write a Letter to Philemon asking him to treat you as a brother in Christ, and I am confident that Philemon will obey what I say he should do out of love." It is a bit shocking for us to hear Paul to say that. But it was not shocking for Onesimus. It was not shocking because he wanted to leave this place and go back to Philemon's household: he had a peace coming from within. After such a long journey, something had changed. He could not explain why or what exactly this change was, but he felt the power of that change flowing from within.

Chapter 9

OBEDIENCE IN LOVE
Do More Than I Say

9.1. INTRODUCTION

One of the main themes of the novel is love conquering worldly values. Javert's worldview is legalistic. He believes in law to the point that he leaves no room for mercy. He believes that he can maintain a better world if everyone obeys the law. He does not accept there is anyone who will love his nephew so much as to steal a loaf of bread for him. He does not believe one who commits a crime will become a good person. He believes that criminals have to be continually monitored by the law and cannot be given any freedom. He does not believe someone will forget and forgive what he did to him. He finally has to choose whether to keep his own world view or accept that there is love in the world. He refused to accept there is love in this world and also found that his old worldview is wrong. He cannot bear this fact and therefore he chooses to die.

The bishop is a believer in love. He sees things differently. With love he sees the potential of Valjean even when Valjean is still full of hatred and steals his precious candle stands. With love he believes Valjean can change, or to put it another way, Valjean can change because the bishop believes in love. The bishop understands well it is only love that can transform a person. It is love that can heal Valjean. It is love that can empower Valjean to live a new life with a new mission. The bishop surely understood there was a possibility that Valjean may choose not to change himself. But it is only in freedom that one can live in mission. But the bishop succeeded.

Love not only brings peace but also struggle. Obedience only comes after genuine struggle because we are living in a world full of values that oppose love. We learned them from our daily participation, unintentionally. We are hurt by these values, or people believing these values, unnoticeably. These values both positive and negative become part of our values over the course of time. Valjean had a deep struggle and so did Javert. Valjean was struggling between hate and love. But one loving word showing the bishop still believed in Valjean's kindness and that he has a soul brought Valjean back to his created image. It is this unreserved and unconditional loving kindness that transformed Valjean. This love was not only an experience but a model and a prototype for Valjean's life. He experienced that power and would like to live out the same even though he needed to resist, face danger, and pay the cost on behalf of others. These are nothing compared to the suffering he had endured from hatred. Valjean obeyed because he experienced love and had a clear idea of faith in his life.

Obedience has no good reputation in our time because obedience usually refers to following an order or an authority we do not really believe in. This is not the obedience the Bible wants us to know. The obedience described in the Bible originates from love, is empowered by love, and is actualized toward love. Obedience to love is a resistance to this world. Maybe that is the same reason Eugene Peterson titled one of his books "subversive spirituality." We are not subversive because we want to subvert something. Our love is subversive because Jesus worked out an incomprehensible model of love for us. Love calls us to follow him.

9.2. INNER TEXTURE: REFRESH "MY HEART"

Yes, brother, let me have this benefit from you in the Lord.
Refresh my heart in Christ. Confident of your obedience, I am
writing to you, knowing that you will do even more than I say.

PHILEMON 20–21

Although vv. 20–21 is the final conclusion of the whole letter, it
still contains strong rhetoric that echoes the theme of the whole
letter. In these two verses, we can find nearly all the key arguments
used in this letter, including brotherhood, a new loving relationship, Onesimus's identity, and freedom in love. Verse 20 starts with
the key relationship, brotherhood. Paul tried very hard to remind
Philemon of the relationship he now has with Onesimus. Lightfoot articulated well that the use of ναί ἀδελφέ is "the entreaty
of a brother to a brother on behalf of a brother."[1] The address of
Philemon as brother again after the request in v. 16 is no accident.

It reminds Philemon twice concerning Onesimus's identity.
Firstly, Paul uses ὀναίμην (onaiman), translated as benefit in the
NRSV, which rhymed with the name Onesimus. Scholars including Lightfoot, Wright, and Dunn agreed that Paul is using a pun
here referring to Onesimus. So when Paul says let me have this
"benefit" from you in the Lord, it can be interpreted as saying let
Paul have "Onesimus" from you. Second, Paul uses σπλάγχνα,
translated as my heart, again. He uses the same term in v. 12 to
refer to Onesimus. When Paul says refresh my heart, the subject
is clearly referring to Onesimus. So what does refresh mean? Paul
used an imperative mood of the word ἀνάπαυσόν (anapauson)
echoing v. 7 in which Paul praised Philemon saying "the hearts
of the saints have been refreshed." The word ἀνάπαυσόν's literal
meaning is "cause to rest" or "to cease with something"[2] In v. 7,
Paul mentioned that it is Philemon's good deed that caused the
"rest" for all saints. What was the good deed here then? What was
the thing that Philemon can help them to rest from? What was

1. Lightfoot, *Saint Paul's Epistles*, 344.
2. Bauernfeind, *TDNT*, 1:350.

Paul burdened with? It should have been clear to Philemon that Onesimus is what Paul cares about and wishes Philemon to take him as a brother in love. In order to emphasize Paul's expectation of how Philemon would treat Onesimus in the new loving relationship, Paul mentioned two core relationships in v. 20 including ὀναίμην in the Lord and σπλάγχνα in Christ.

Paul did not specify the concrete action Philemon should take. This said, Paul's request is clear: accept Onesimus as a beloved brother. However, Paul mentioned in v. 14 that he really wants Philemon to respond to Paul's request out of love rather than out of force. How should Philemon respond then? In light of the tension between freedom and expectation, Paul says he was "Confident in your obedience" in v. 21.

The Greek word for "confident of" can also be interpreted as "persuaded by or convinced by something concrete." This view echoes Paul's saying in v. 5 that Paul has heard what Philemon has done in love and through faith. What Philemon had done surely demonstrates that he did follow the principal of love and faith. This voluntary following God's teaching and working out his faith is exactly what Paul's understanding of obedience all about. This obedience must be come from one's free will not from force or other means. Obedience is what Paul expects Philemon to respond with because the Greek word for obedience is ὑπακοή (hupakoe), which comes from the verb ὑπακούω (hupakouo), composed of a preposition ὑπο and a verb ακούω (akouo), meaning I hear. So the basic meaning of ὑπακούω is rooted in hearing. This hearing refers more to "children, slaves or wives who stand in a divinely willed relationship of subordination.[3]" The word suggests a kind of heartfelt submission to an authority figure. This is exactly what Paul hoped to have from Philemon. A choice to hear the right voice. A choice made not out of obligation or pressure, but out of this kind of heartfelt obedience. The outcome, then, would not be a minimum response. That is the reason Paul added "knowing that you will do more than what I say." This "knowing" becomes a rhetorical

3. Kittel, *TDNT*, 223.

reminder to Philemon to think one step further concerning what he can do for Onesimus out of love and faith in Christ.

9.3. INTERTEXTUAL TEXTURE: EXPECTATION OF RESPONSE, OBEDIENCE IN FREEDOM

Obedience in Paul's mind is not just following order. It is following the authority figure's mindset, values and model wholeheartedly. It will have more impact than just using one's hieratical power. That may be the reason why Paul put obedience ὑπακοή in a close relationship with faith. He uses the words ὑπακοὴν πίστεως (*hupakoan pisteos*) twice, translated as obedience to faith, in Rom 1:5 and 16:26. Paul praised Philemon's faith and prayed that his faith could be effective in Christ in vv. 5–6 of the Letter to Philemon. The final remark actually echoes these two verses. In order to make his faith effective, Philemon has to respond in an obedient way.

What is obedience to faith? It implies the willingness to resist present values and listen to God's voice and teaching. As faith has to be worked out through love, obedience refers to one's choice of working it out in spite of all the strong prevailing values. It is always difficult to refuse to follow the prevailing values either in Roman times or in our capitalist society because you have to bear the cost of doing so. You will have to forgo personal interests including honor and monetary return. So that the drive to be obedient must not come from outside but from within nor from a calculation of cost and benefit but from love. Paul had such experiences and mentioned them in quite some detail in Philippians 3. Before Paul mentions his own transformation, in ch. 2, after introducing the countercultural values of a Christian, he introduces Jesus' humble model of forgoing what he deserves to have and his voluntary choice to serve us as in the image of slave. He then mentions the Philippians' obedience again telling them that they have always obeyed (v. 12) because "it is God who is at work in you, enabling you both to will and to work for his good pleasure" (v. 13). This obedience is not one's personal decision but the consequence of faith. This obedience to faith enables one to do good even in the face of strong countercultural challenges.

The Philippians were facing challenges from the Roman values which were greatly self-seeking and in direct opposition to Christ's self-sacrificing neighbor-loving model. We can grasp Paul's worry about these challenging values all over the letter, including the envy and rivalry in 1:15, selfish ambition in 1:17 and 2:3, looking after one's own interests in 2:4, seeking their own interests in 2:21, and "their end is destruction; their god is the belly; and their glory is their shame; their minds are set on earthly things" in 3:19. Therefore, obedience is not context free. Philippians 1:27 can well articulate the full meaning of obedience in Paul's mind as he says, "Live your life in a manner worthy of the gospel of Christ, so that, whether I come and see you or am absent and hear about you, I will know that you are standing firm in one spirit, striving side by side with one mind for the faith of the gospel." On the one hand, Paul reminded them to live out a life with its value based on the gospel of Christ, which implies having countercultural values. On the other hand, similar to what is said in 2:12 when he talked about "you have obeyed," he also mentions "no matter with or without his presence." We can see that in Paul's mind, a genuine living out of the gospel is a kind of obedience to faith in which Christians are willingly living out the value of Christ with their "one mind for the faith of the gospel."

Reflecting on Paul's concept of obedience, we can comprehend the whole of Paul's ethical thoughts from the key concepts we have discussed in previous chapters. Paul does not only want things to be done, but he also wants the transformation of Christians, and therefore, obedience out of faith in love. The whole letter should be read from an eschatological perspective which will remind us that we have heavenly citizenship while still living in this present sinful world. With that, love brings us new identity and power to live in this eschatological world. So when Paul says he would rather beg Philemon based on love he is actually referring to this new power. With this new identity, members of the believing community are all in a new relationship with each other, called brotherhood. Also, because of God's loving salvation, we are free from the bondage of this world and free to love. With our new identity, this freedom to love is also our new mission to live out in this world. Therefore, Paul does not expect someone to have to be forced to do anything, but expects one to freely respond out of one's new identity of love.

9.4. NARRATIVE EIGHT: RETURNING AND HEALING

Onesimus took the same road he had traveled when he left Philemon and tried to find Paul. Yet, it was not the same experience as when he walked on that same road before. He was less burdened now, even though he knew he might have to face punishment or go back to being a slave if Philemon did not listen to Paul. Onesimus had something new in him; he wondered whether it was what Paul and Timothy described as faith. He remembered what Jesus had done for him. He remembered his own feeling of freedom when he started to accept Jesus as his Lord. He remembered the satisfaction he felt when he worked for Paul, Timothy, and Festus with a mission of love. He remembered his own change and had confidence that Philemon would follow Paul's reminder, even though he did not read the letter. He had faith in Paul and in Jesus.

When he finally returned to Philemon's household, he did face a moment of hesitation over whether he had to go back. But the hesitation disappeared quickly, and he walked slowly into the house. He saw his two friends, Chrestus and Aratos, standing in the dining room. You could tell from their eyes that they wanted to come give a big hug to Onesimus because they had thought they might never see him again. However, they had to hold back their emotions to avoid being treated as a conspirator of Onesimus. He could also see the worry in their eyes. There was no need to explain what they were worried about, and Onesimus knew that too. He walked toward Chrestus and asked him to give the letter to Philemon, who was taking an afternoon nap. Onesimus could do nothing but wait.

After about an hour or two, Chrestus came out, followed by Philemon. The atmosphere in the room was very tense, and everyone in the room was very nervous, except Onesimus. His peaceful expression surprised everyone, but Onesimus knew where this peace had come from. Philemon walked directly to Onesimus, which was not a normal gesture for a master. When he walked closer, Onesimus could tell he had been crying not long ago. "You had the freedom to walk away, but you chose to come back and bring me this precious letter. Thank you for trusting me and coming back home, brother. Your faith is greater than mine. I am so sorry that I have used the world's values to treat you badly; now I have to repent." After saying these words to Onesimus, Philemon spoke to the others: "Please ask everyone in this household to come here."

When the members of the household arrived in the atrium, they were all surprised to see Onesimus there standing next to Philemon without any hint that Philemon was going to punish him. Philemon invited everyone to listen to the letter Paul had written to him: "Paul, a prisoner of Christ Jesus, and Timothy our brother . . . Confident of your obedience, I am writing to you, knowing that you will do even more than I say. One thing more—prepare a guest room for me, for I am hoping through your prayers to be restored to you." This was the first time Onesimus heard the letter. He started to cry when he heard Paul say, "He is my begotten son, my heart and our beloved brother." He cried because Paul had announced that he was not a slave through Philemon's mouth, which brought ultimate healing to Onesimus. Although Paul had never treated him as a slave, hearing that he was not and was instead a precious son and Paul's heart was another story. This letter was a letter of healing not only to Onesimus but also to Philemon. Living as a master under Roman rules, he did not see all his slaves, nor his clients, as genuine human beings. There was only self-benefit and self-interest in Philemon's eyes. This selfishness had isolated him from his neighbors and the love of God, because the love of God is not for our "self," only for our neighbor. In order to taste the fruitfulness of God's love, we have to reconnect with our neighbor.

Thus Paul's letter to Philemon was not only for Onesimus's sake but also for Philemon's. It did not only bring healing to Onesimus but also to Philemon.

Chapter 10

THE RHETORIC OF THE LETTER

A Love Message to Be Heard

10.1. INTRODUCTION

This chapter is the concluding chapter of this book. However, I am not going to repeat the messages of the previous chapters. Instead, I will discuss one hidden but very important purpose of the letter. Paul crafted the Letter to Philemon with great care and love. Paul did not only want to tell Philemon what is right to do, but also wanted his messages to be heard. A right message is good but only a heard message will be effective. He did not only tell Philemon what to do but told him to act out what he believed was a model for Philemon. This spirituality is essential to Christianity. However, this world tries very hard to discourage us from holding this belief. The giant Roman slavery machine and capitalism have penetrated into every part of our lives. There is a large number of people who have a vested interest in the current social system. The whole of society is and was built upon these systems. This grandness and immovability will easily kill our passion to speak anything against it because it seems that whatever we do will be in vain. However, that is just not the spirituality of Christianity. Christianity's hope does not depend on whether we can change the reality instantly or not, but depends on our faith in Jesus' teaching and example.

10.2. SPIRITUALITY OF RHETORIC

The threat of living under the control of an empire is that we may gradually believe that there is nothing we can do to make a difference. We cannot change the policy. We cannot change the government and we cannot change the rules of the dirty political game. Yes, we may not be able to bring big change to this political reality. On the other hand, people find it so difficult to listen to a voice of love. They are so adapted to the present world. The voice of Jesus and the Bible sound so strange to them. These problems are all real, but they are also our calling as well. Christians make a great mistake in thinking that people are so willing to listen to the truth about love. It is the other way round. They don't really want to hear and that is exactly the reason they desperately need it.

To keep speaking about the gospel and trying to use every different method to make people hear God's message is a spiritual calling. It is the spirituality we can observe in Jesus as well as in all the New Testament writers. They used different kinds of rhetoric hoping to open their audience's hearts so the audience would listen to their message. The Bible writers, or our God, did not only write down something they thought God thinks is right, or doctrine concerning things that you need to do. Nor did they write down the price list of your wrongdoing only to threaten the readers. Rhetoric is composed of narratives, testimonies, metaphors, parables, teaching, direct sayings, inter-dialogue with the Hebrew Bible and other contemporary texts, puns, rhymes, and various kinds of poetic structure. We usually refer to these kinds of skills as rhetoric. Rhetoric did not originate from Christianity. It was a part of the Greco-Roman culture. At the time of the Roman Republic, both civilizations depended on the public's honor and authorization for important issues. Patricians or senates needed someone to help them to persuade people to accept their policy.

So they employed orators to help them to write or give speeches. Some senators had very good rhetorical skills. The most famous one is surely Cicero.

Biblical scholars, like George Kennedy and Vernon Robbins, are among the earliest scholars who discover the rhetorical elements in the New Testament. They started to investigate the relevant rhetoric elements in the New Testament and found that there is not only classical rhetoric in it as New Testament writers did invent new rhetorical skills based on their theology and context. Paul is one of them. He not only made use of classical rhetoric but also invented new forms. As Christians, we should not only appreciate rhetoric as a literal skill or theology, but also the spirituality behind it. In this book, I hope I have been able to demonstrate to you how eagerly Paul tried to make his messages be heard by Philemon. In fact, he does not only care about Philemon but also Onesimus. His message speaks also to Onesimus as well.

Rhetoric in Hope

The use of rhetoric reflects Paul's hope. This hope is anchored in his faith, not the possibility of changing the reality. Christians should not be unrealistic, but neither should they be too realistic. Ignorance about reality will make our faith irrelevant to this world. Putting too much emphasize on the darkness of reality will discourage us from speaking up for truth. Paul's eschatological thought reminds us to stand on reality and look up to our heavenly identity and calling. Paul knew how difficult it would be for Philemon to follow his advice because the influence of Roman slavery was so grand. It would not have been realistic for Paul to think that the slavery system would break down quickly or easily in his lifetime. So what was Paul's hope? Paul's hope was based on God's calling. We have hope because it is what God calls us to. We have hope because Jesus demonstrated the model for us. We have hope because we see the little gap that provides enough room for us to actualize our calling.

Rhetoric in Love

Rhetoric is not only a skill but a reflection of the deep beliefs of one person. It is especially true in Paul's case because unlike the orators of his time, he was not speaking on behalf of those who were more highly honored, nor did he speak for his own benefit. He was speaking for a slave whose social status was at the bottom of Roman society. Notwithstanding, Paul knew full well how difficult it could be for Philemon to follow his request. He knew it was not an easy task. Paul also knew how deeply Onesimus had been hurt and how difficult healing could be. Paul surely realized that it was beyond his ability to bring any change to worldly institutions. But then, why did he still speak? It could be in vain. Paul could have lost an important friend, brother, and supporter. It is only because of love. It is the love he experienced when he met Jesus. This love totally transformed him, turning his value system upside down. He says, "Yet whatever gains I had, these I have come to regard as loss because of Christ" (Phil 3:7). He knew how powerful this love could be. Once you have experienced that love you will not be the same. Believing in love, Paul writes this letter in love. Every word he writes is because of love. It is love that gives him the unconventional perspective of deeply believing a slave was a brother. You can sense the power of love from how hard Paul has tried to strike for room, no matter how little is it, to speak for Onesimus. You can feel Paul's passion also. Because of his love for Onesimus, he writes this letter. Because he still believed in the transformative power of love, he chose to beg Philemon in love rather than use hierarchical power.

Rhetoric in Resistance

Paul's use of rhetoric is a kind of resistance. Resistance could have many forms. It does not necessarily appear as direct confrontation nor originate from hatred. It could be resistance done in a loving way if we have a correct understanding of love. The rhetoric in the Letter to Philemon is a masterpiece of this kind of resistance.

This kind of resistance does not aim to overthrow the system at once, but to preserve and nurture the heavenly values that we are called to live with. The insistence on living out those values reflects Paul's disagreement with the system and its underlying values. It reflects his heavenly identity and worldly concern. Paul saw a transcendent relationship with Onesimus as a beloved brother. However, he also understood how deep the worldly relationship had penetrated every part of Roman society. He did not overlook the reality and the associated difficulties. Therefore, he chose to use rhetoric to open the eyes of Philemon so that he could see, to warm his heart so that Philemon can feel, and, most important of all, to move Philemon so that he can finally listen to Paul's request that Onesimus be treated not as a slave but as a beloved brother. In that time of great suppression, to keep on using rhetoric may have been the most powerful form of resistance possible at that historical moment.

Rhetoric in Reconciliation

Saying that rhetoric is a kind of resistance does not imply that resistance is the purpose of it. Resistance is not the purpose, but reconciliation is. Love let Paul see the brokenness of this world and in Philemon and Onesimus. This seeing became Paul's mission in writing this letter. One clear goal was to help Philemon reconcile with God, the believing community, and Onesimus. Without love, Philemon could not taste the fruit of the reconciliation. Reconciliation goes back to the created relationship. That is the message of the gospel and what Jesus died for. As Paul says in 2 Cor 5:18–19, "All this is from God, who reconciled us to himself through Christ, and has given us the ministry of reconciliation; that is, in Christ God was reconciling the world to himself, not counting their trespasses against them, and entrusting the message of reconciliation to us." We are not only being reconciled but are called to be the agents of reconciliation.

Paul did not only want Philemon to have full reconciliation, but he also wanted Onesimus to be reconciled with God, himself, and the world. They both suffered from the brokenness of the world but in different ways. Philemon's brokenness comes from his adoption of worldly values and therefore created a great gap between him and the world. Conversely, Onesimus's hurt and brokenness was caused by these worldly values. Paul's rhetoric is not only for Philemon but also for the healing of Onesimus. In order to appreciate the complete rhetoric of the letter, we should also be aware that Onesimus will be one of the readers of the letter. Either he read it before he decided to go back to Philemon's household, or he was in the audience when Philemon read the letter to all members of his household church. With this special audience in mind, we can better hear Paul's rhetoric.

Besides the above, all the rhetoric elaborated and was aimed at asking Philemon to receive Onesimus as a brother. Some verses can also be read as rhetoric intended to heal Onesimus. When he calls Onesimus my child and my heart, it heals Onesimus's broken self-identity. It may have been the first time he heard publicly that he is neither a thing, nor does he only have value as an instrument. More than that, the letter was written by a respected person with high honor. When he heard the whole letter and Paul's final request to Philemon saying that he is "no longer a slave but more than a slave, a beloved brother," I do believe Onesimus could feel Paul's love for him. It is unconventional love. A love that transcends all social values and sees him as a genuine human being and brother.

Rhetoric in Faith in Action

Besides all the rhetoric in the wordings, one of the most powerful pieces of rhetoric in the letter is the letter itself. The existence of the letter reflects Paul's faith in action. He did not only teach others to love one's neighbor as oneself, but to act out this teaching. He could have just prayed for Onesimus or comforted him and that's all. The willingness to write such a letter reveals Paul had not submitted to the prevailing values. Paul really treated Onesimus as his beloved brother. He tried his best to persuade Philemon to accept his heavenly value. It is a letter of faith in action. It is his faith in God and Philemon that gave him the power to write. It is love that motivated him to write. This is exactly what "faith working through love" means.

10.3. ENDING NARRATIVE

This book is filled with different narratives. Different characters and scenes in *Les Misérables* help introduce us to different themes in each chapter because we know well the complications of these characters and the background of the novel. Also, there are so many similarities between the context of *Les Misérables*, the Roman Empire, and our capitalist society. From different scenes in the movie, we can easily appreciate different values and tensions that may be difficult to introduce without the help the narrative.

There is a made-up story at the end of each chapter to help readers better understand the historical context of Roman slavery. The reason for doing so is we do not only need historical facts but imagination in order to understand the complicated world of Roman slavery. Roman slavery was not only composed of masters and slaves but complicated formal and informal institutions. These complicated institutions will produce complicated feelings and perceptions as well as intricate relationships between masters and slaves. The creative narrative serves as an imaginative setting to help readers not only understand the characteristics of Roman slavery but also the subsequent master-slave relationships and psychological aspects of them.

At the end of this book, we need one more narrative to help us to imagine the ending of the Philemon-Onesimus relationship. What did Philemon do with Onesimus? Did he free him? Did Philemon restore the beloved brotherhood relationship with Onesimus? How? We have to admit that we do not have any direct historical evidence that tells a definite ending. However, we can use a story to help us to imagine one. This is not exactly a story, but a rumor from the early second century. In Ignatius's letter to the Ephesians, he mentioned a name who was the bishop of Ephesus, and his name is Onesimus. In the letter Ignatius wrote: "I received, therefore, your whole multitude in the name of God, through Onesimus, a man of inexpressible love and your bishop in the flesh, whom I pray you by Jesus Christ to love, and that you would all seek to be like him." Although we may not be one hundred percent sure whether this Onesimus is the Onesimus in the Letter to Philemon, we can still make a reasonable guess. First, if Onesimus had not trusted Philemon and Paul, he would have really run away with the letter. Second, if Philemon did not agree with Paul after reading the letter, he would probably not have kept a letter he did not agree with. Thirdly, this letter was kept and it became part of the canon of the New Testament. It must have concerned someone important or the testimony of it was so strong that it had spread widely so that the church fathers had no excuse to exclude it from the canon. Finally, given the side evidence from Ignatius, this Onesimus was a man of inexpressible love. This loving character should remind us about the bishop in *Les Misérables* and Valjean. Also, we should be able to hear the echo of how heavily Paul emphasized the importance of love in the letter. It makes perfect sense for this Onesimus to be the same Onesimus as the one in Paul's letter. It is not a wishful thinking but a faithful imagination.

BIBLIOGRAPHY

Callahan, Allan. "Paul's Epistle to Philemon: Toward an Alternative Argumentum." *Harvard Theological Review* 86 (1993) 357–76.

Dunn, James D. G. *Romans*. WBC 38B. Dallas: Word, 1998.

———. *The Theology of Paul the Apostle*. Grand Rapids: Eerdmans, 1998.

Fitzmyer, Joseph A. *Romans: A New Translation with Introduction and Commentary*. The Anchor Bible 33. New York: Doubleday, 1993.

———. *The Letter to Philemon*. Anchor Bible 34C. New York: Doubleday, 2000.

Furnish, Paul Victor. *Theology and Ethics in Paul*. Louisville: John Knox, 2009.

Garnsey Peter. *Ideas of Slavery from Aristotle to Augustine*. Cambridge: Cambridge University Press, 1996.

Hellerman, Joseph. *Philippians: Exegetical Guide to the Greek New Testament*. Nashville: B&H Academic, 2015.

Ip, Alex Hon Ho. *A Socio-Rhetorical Interpretation of the Letter to Philemon in Light of the New Institutional Economics: An Exhortation to Transform a Master-Slave Economic Relationship into a Brotherly Loving Relationship*. Tübingen: Mohr Siebeck, 2017.

Kittel, Bromiley, et al. *TDNT*. Grand Rapids: Eerdmans, 1964.

Knox, John. *Philemon among the Letters of Paul*. New York: Abingdon, 1959.

Lightfoot, Joseph B. *Saint Paul's Epistles to the Colossians and to Philemon: A Revised Test with Introduction, Notes, and Dissertations*. Reprint. Peabody, MA: Hendrickson, 1993.

Marrow, Stanley B. "Parrhesia and the New Testament." *Catholic Biblical Quarterly* 44 (1982) 431–46.

O'Brien, Peter. *Colossians, Philemon*. WBC 44. Dallas: Nelson, 1998.

Petersen, Norman. *Rediscovering Paul: Philemon and the Sociological World of Paul's Narrative World*. Eugene, OR: Wipf & Stock.

Sampley, Paul. *Pauline Partnership in Christ*. Philadelphia: Fortress, 1980.

Schubert, Paul. *Form and Function of the Pauline Thanksgiving*. Beihefte zur Zritschrift für die neutestamentliche Wissenschaft 20. Berlin: de Gruyter, 1939.

Thiselton, Anthony C. *The Living Paul: An Introduction to the Apostle's Life and Thought*. Downers Grove: InterVarsity, 2009.

Robbins, Vernon K. *Exploring the Texture of Texts: A Guide to Socio-Rhetorical Interpretations.* Valley Forge, PA : Trinity, 1996.

————. *The Tapestry of Early Christian Discourse: Rhetoric, Society and Ideology.* New York: Routledge, 1996.

Winter, Sara. "Methodological Observations on a New Interpretation of Paul's Letter to Philemon." *Union Seminary Quarterly Review* 39 (1984) 203–12.

Wolter, Michael. *Paul: An Outline of His Theology.* Waco, TX: Baylor University Press, 2015.